Ministry Team
TRAINING MANUAL

Randy Clark

Global Awakening Ministry Team Training Manual

©Copyright 2004, 2018 Randy Clark

Apostolic Network of Global Awakening (ANGA)
1451 Clark Street
Mechanicsburg, PA 17055

Tenth Printing with updates: August 2018

ISBN: 978-1-944238-18-6

TABLE OF CONTENTS

INTRODUCTION

This training manual is written for those who have a desire and a calling from God to be involved in ministry to needy, hurting people – in a crusade setting, in a local church, or across the kitchen table!

The purpose of this manual is to give some basic, practical instruction on praying for the needs of others in specific ways. It contains general instructions for ministering, praying for salvation, praying for the sick, and praying for deliverance from curses and from demonic oppression. The manual is designed for use either as an aid in classroom teaching situations, or by an individual who wishes to self-study and begin to help others on his own.

There are different ways of praying for specific needs. It is not intended to suggest that the methods described in this manual are necessarily the best methods. However, they are sound. The beginner who uses the methods suggested here will not go far astray in his ministry. He will see success in his ministry and will discover that the Holy Spirit will use him as people he prays for are healed or show improvement. He will not cause emotional or other damage to the persons he prays for.

There is no substitute for experience in praying for healing and deliverance. If one can attend a class where clinic time – actual practice – is offered, or if one can join with another who is experienced in such ministry, he should take advantage of such opportunities. However, the Holy Spirit Himself is a wonderful teacher and has a desire to help anyone who cannot gain experience in any way other than by stepping out in prayer himself. Even those with experience must depend greatly on the guiding hand of the Spirit in their ministries.

This training manual is intended primarily for those who will be involved in one-on-one prayer for the needy person, rather than in group praying. It presumes that if two or three are praying, they will follow a bit of structure, with one person praying at a time and the others interceding, rather than having both or all three praying at once.

Although it is not explicitly stated here, pray-ers are encouraged to be attentive to the prayers of others for physical healing, inner healing, deliverance, salvation, and the like. He may notice ways of praying that seem to be more effective than his own. When that happens, the beginner should have no reluctance to emulate the other. No one has a patent on particular ways of praying. It is good for each member of the body of Christ to learn from the others, to constantly seek more effective ways to minister, and to help those who may be less experienced than he is.

It is not in the scope of this manual to consider a ministry that involves rebuke, accusation, the giving of directions, or personal prophecy. It is not in the scope of this manual to consider providing counseling, medical advice, or other in-depth ministry. If the person providing ministry senses that rebuke or correction is needed, or that counseling or medical assistance is needed, he should refer the one receiving ministry to an appropriate, trained person who can provide the needed assistance.

Much of the material in this manual relates to method – to ways of praying and ministering. However, as noted frequently in these pages, it cannot be stated too strongly that the most important aspect of any ministry is to be a channel for the love of God to flow into the person receiving ministry. Without love, even a powerful ministry is empty, regardless of apparent success. A person who receives loving ministry is blessed, even though he may not receive a particular healing. Everyone reading this manual is capable of being a channel of God's love.

A second important aspect of ministry is to be a channel for the Spirit and Life of Jesus to be poured into the person for whom one is praying. The Holy Spirit is alive and very creative. He will powerfully use those who learn to hear His voice and follow His leading when ministering to needy and spiritually hungry people.

It is our hope that this manual will be a springboard for you from which to launch into a life of effective, powerful ministry and discover the wonderful resources God has provided for us through His Holy Spirit.

Throughout this manual we have used masculine forms (man, men) and pronouns (he, him, his) to avoid cumbersome grammar. They are used in an inclusive sense and are in no way intended to exclude our precious sisters in the Lord.

1 CORINTHIANS 13:1-2
Though I speak with the tongues of men and of angels, but have not love, I have become as sounding brass or a clanging cymbal. And though I have the gift of prophecy, and understand all mysteries and all knowledge, and though I have all faith, so that I could remove mountains, but have not love, I am nothing.

1 CORINTHIANS 13:13
And now abide faith, hope, love, these three; but the greatest of these is love.

1 JOHN 4:7-8 (AMPLIFIED BIBLE)
Beloved, let us love ... for love is of God. He who does not love does not know God, for God is love.

JOHN 7:38
From his innermost being shall flow (continually) springs and rivers of living water.

I want to express my personal thanks to John and Melly Mackenzie for their substantial contributions to the writing of this manual.

Dr Randy Clark

Chapter 1
MINISTRY TEAM PROTOCOL

SERVING ON A MINISTRY TEAM

Among the objectives of the person who serves on a ministry team, in a church, in a "healing room" situation, at a crusade, as a member of a visiting team to a different church or meeting, should be the following:

> To facilitate the moving of the Holy Spirit under the direction of the pastoral or other appointed leadership of the team.
>
> To provide mature ministry direction through order, safety and cooperation.
>
> To avoid confusion, offense and harm.
>
> As an individual ministering as part of the team, among his objectives should be:
>
> To release God's love, healing, empowerment and deliverance to those who indicate a desire to receive prayer.
>
> To edify, exhort, and comfort.

It is not the purpose of a ministry team (or any member of the team) to release rebuke or correction, or to give direction.

It is not the purpose to provide counseling or other in-depth ministry involvement.

This manual contains simple guidelines based on Biblical principles to help bring greater fruitfulness to ministry time.

SERVING AS A TEAM MEMBER AT A CONFERENCE OR OTHER SCHEDULED MEETING

The unity of the team members and the team leadership is a critical factor in the effectiveness of any ministry team. Each team member will be expected to:

> Minister within the guidelines established by the pastoral leadership of the meeting.
>
> Cheerfully submit to and be loyal to the pastoral leadership of the meeting.
>
> Lay aside his own ministry pattern and follow the pattern established for the meeting.
>
> Pray regularly for the scheduled meetings.
>
> Attend scheduled prayer sessions prior to meetings.
>
> Intercede for God's anointing on the worship team.

Intercede for God's anointing on the preacher or speakers.

Intercede for God's love to be manifest in others and in himself.

Intercede for the presence of the Holy Spirit.

Intercede for an open spirit to recognize words of wisdom, words of knowledge and discernment given by the Holy Spirit.

Step down as a team member if requested to do so by the leadership.

QUALIFICATIONS OF A MINISTRY TEAM MEMBER

The qualifications of a ministry team member will be set by the person(s) responsible for the church service or conference meeting or other setting where the ministry will take place. There may be particular requirements for a particular organization or setting. In general, any ministry team member must be born again (John 3:3, Romans 6:23), be a member of a local church and subject to the leadership of that church.

Depending on the circumstances, such as for a conference, a team member may be required to obtain his or her pastor's written approval to serve on the team and may be asked to file an application to serve on the ministry team. If there are training sessions involved, the person wishing to serve should make it a point to attend all training sessions unless excused.

DESIRABLE QUALITIES OF A MINISTRY TEAM MEMBER

None of us are perfect, but we are enjoined by the Lord to strive for perfection (Matt 5:48). Accordingly, a ministry team member should be making some progress in achieving desirable qualities in his personal life. This basically means he should be consciously allowing God to change and build his character. Some of these desirable qualities are:

A SERVANT'S HEART

Humility. (Proverbs 3:34, James 4:6, 1 Peter 5:5)

Obedience. (John 14:23, 15:10)

Freedom from desire for recognition.

Faithfulness. (1 Timothy 1:12-14)

Willingness to continue ministry to the end of a meeting.

A TEACHABLE SPIRIT

Willingness to receive ministry as well as to give ministry.

Willingness to accept correction.

DEMONSTRATING CERTAIN LIFESTYLE CHARACTERISTICS

The most important single element in ministry is one's relationship with God. Unless your relationship to God is free from rebellion, anger and intentional disobedience, you should make corrections in your own lifestyle before attempting to minister to others. Some characteristics of a person who has a close relationship with God are the following:

Spending time daily with God in praise, worship and adoration.

Spending time in regular reading and study of the scriptures.

Walking in forgiveness as a lifestyle. (Matthew 6:14-15, 18:21-22; 2 Corinthians 2:10-11)

Walking in repentance as a lifestyle. (Matthew 3:2, Luke 13:3, Revelations 3:19)

Practicing continually being re-filled with the Holy Spirit. (Acts 4:31, 13:9; Ephesians 5:18)

Growing in demonstration of the fruit of the Spirit in his life. (See Galatians 5:22)

LOVE	**PATIENCE**	**GENTLENESS**
JOY	**KINDNESS**	**FAITHFULNESS**
PEACE	**GOODNESS**	**SELF-CONTROL**

Practicing obedience to the leading of the Holy Spirit. (Romans 8:14)

Faithfulness in carrying out any ministry currently assigned by the Lord.

Peer recognition as a godly person.

Making extraordinary effort to avoid sin.

Denominational and racial neutrality in ministering.

A calling from God to serve in this capacity.

No one except you can tell whether you meet all of these characteristics. But you probably can tell and people who know you well are likely to have observations about some of these characteristics. A periodic review of the above list may be helpful to you in developing your own relationship with God.

OTHER DESIRABLE ELEMENTS OF CHARACTER

Reasonable Biblical knowledge. (1 Timothy 4:6-7, 2 Timothy 2:15, 3:16)

A person of prayer. (Ephesians 6:18)

A stable person, with good judgment.

Free from panic, fear and worry. (2 Timothy 1:7, Phillipians 4:6-7)

Able to manage his personal finances.

Able to withstand spiritual attacks that may follow service to the Lord.

So aware of God's love for himself, that he can assure others of God's love for them.

A ministry team member should appreciate that the kind of person he is – how he lives and what he does in daily life – is more important than what he says and does in ministry.

> **JAMES 4:6**
> BUT HE GIVES MORE GRACE. THEREFORE HE SAYS, "GOD RESISTS THE PROUD, BUT GIVES GRACE TO THE HUMBLE."
>
> **HEBREWS 4:16**
> LET US THEREFORE COME BOLDLY TO THE THRONE OF GRACE, THAT WE MAY OBTAIN MERCY AND FIND GRACE TO HELP IN TIME OF NEED.

GUIDELINES AND POLICIES

The following are general guidelines and policies associated with serving on a ministry team. Please read them carefully.

ADMINISTRATION

Always comply with the directions given by those in authority for the meeting or the place where ministry is to take place. These will usually be the pastor of the church where you are ministering, or the leader of the meeting where you are serving, or their representatives.

You may be asked to wear a name tag identifying you as a ministry team member.

You may be asked not to minister without another ministry team member and a catcher.

CATCHERS

Catching is an important aspect of Holy Spirit renewal ministry. It allows people to freely receive and rest in the anointing without the fear of getting hurt. Also, it helps keep the ministry time "decent and in order" (1 Corinthians 14:40). In addition, it is a great training opportunity for those wanting to join the ministry team or expand their prayer ministry skills. As a catcher, keep the following in mind:

When preparing to catch someone, keep your elbows close to your sides. Place your hands near the small of the person's back and gently touch his back or shoulder. This gives the person confidence that you are there and does not interfere with the prayer process. Have one foot slightly ahead of the other so you are balanced. Attempt to move back with the person, allowing your hands to slide up the person's back as he falls, rather than trying to take his whole weight upon yourself.

Be careful to protect yourself from injury. Be balanced, alert and aware of the floor space around you. Be sure there is space on the floor to let the person down if he falls. If there isn't, move to a better place.

Request assistance if the person's size or weight is more than you can manage.

Be watchful and alert as people begin to sway under the anointing, including people around you who are not being prayed for at the time.

Periodically, lightly touch the person you are prepared to catch in the middle back or on the shoulder to assure him or her that you are still there.

Pay attention to the task at hand so you are "right there" when you are needed. It is discouraging to the person praying when he or she realizes that you are not there at a crucial moment. If you become tired, or if it's time for your own ministry, tell the person praying and recruit someone else.

If you have a physical injury or disability, please do not volunteer to catch.

When available, use cloths to cover a person's exposed areas such as legs above the knees and midriffs.

THINGS TO AVOID

Pushing or pulling anyone over – this will reduce the confidence in your ministry on the part of those to whom you minister.

Holding anyone up by grabbing the shoulders or upper back.

Rubbing or touching in ways that might be annoying or misconstrued.

SAME-GENDER PRAYER POLICY

Concerning ministry to persons of the opposite sex, follow the policy of the leadership of the meeting.

Try to have women minister to women and men to men. In any event, do not minister alone (alone in a room, or so far from others in a large room that you cannot be heard) to someone of the opposite sex.

In deliverance ministry, the ministry team should always have at least one person of the same sex as the person receiving ministry.

LAYING-ON OF HANDS

The appropriate places to lay hands on someone for general prayer are the forehead and hands. Apply a soft touch, being sensitive to not offend anyone.

When praying for healing, if the affected part of the prayee's body is not a sensitive one -- for example, if it is his foot, ankle, elbow, back, neck, eyes, etc. -- the ministry team member may touch the affected part. This sometimes seems to bring the power of the Holy Spirit in you closer to the point where healing is needed. If the problem is in a sensitive spot such as in the abdomen, the ministry team member can ask the person receiving ministry to put his hand on the affected part and then place his own hand on the hand of the prayee. If even this does not seem appropriate, simply hold the person's hand lightly or touch his forehead lightly as you pray.

HYGIENE

Ministering at the altar is demanding and often physically taxing. Start fresh, use deodorant beforehand, and make sure you have plenty of breath mints available.

INJURIES

If a person is injured in any way, stop ministering and tend to the person's physical needs. Notify a supervisor or pastor as soon as possible.

COMPLAINTS

Remember that we are working as a team. The pastoral leadership handles any complaints about how you minister to an individual as follows:

Someone in leadership will personally contact you.

The leader will explain the complaint to you as it was explained to him or her.

You may explain your side of the situation.

Together you discuss possible solutions.

If necessary, the leader will ask you to step down from the ministry team.

QUIETNESS IN THE MINISTRY AREA

Always talk quietly in the ministry area. When you finish praying, be aware that non-prayer fellowship and conversation in the ministry area may distract those still receiving ministry.

If it is practicable to do so, suggest that music during prayer ministry be quiet and worshipful.

THE GOAL

The goal in ministry is not to see a visible manifestation of some kind. Though that may happen, it is not our goal. The goal is an impartation of the love of God through you, and a release of the power of the Holy Spirit in the name of Jesus.

MINISTRY TEAM PRAYER NEEDS

Pray daily for yourself and ministry team members as the Holy Spirit prompts you. Items to pray for include the following:

The whole armor of God according to Ephesians 6:12-17.

The blood of Jesus covering family, home and property.

A hedge of protection to fill in any gaps.

All things to come under God's authority and obedience as in 2 Corinthians 10:4-5.

Discernment to recognize our adversary, the devil, who comes to accuse and bring condemnation and guilt, unlike John 3:17.

God's favor and blessings according to Luke 2:52.

Unity in relationships in all arenas of life, leaving no room for the enemy to bring division and not taking on others' offenses, as in Psalm 133.

A free-flowing spirit of forgiveness.

The spread of life-giving words as seeds of righteousness and clear communication.

Grateful and humble hearts toward God and others.

Teachable, cooperative and flexible spirits.

God's grace for the task and for one another.

Peace -- that everyone find his or her secret place at Jesus' feet daily.

A fresh anointing to flow during the day and throughout the meetings while performing respective tasks.

God's personal work in each individual through his or her ministry to be made like Christ.

That God will be exalted -- His kingdom come, His will be done, His glory filling each one.

That the joy of the Lord will be their strength for overcoming physical exhaustion and insomnia.

Wisdom from above and for "God thoughts" according to James 1:5.

Love like that described in 1 Corinthians 13:2-3 and Romans 5:5.

A TEAM MOTTO
BE FRIENDLY!
BE FLEXIBLE!
PRAY EARNESTLY!
HAVE GOOD BREATH!

Chapter 2
PRAYER GUIDELINES

PERSONAL LIFESTYLE AND PREPARATION

BE A CHANNEL FOR THE LOVE OF GOD AND THE COMFORT AND POWER OF THE HOLY SPIRIT

Without the love of God, and without the help of the Holy Spirit, you can do little that will be of long-term benefit to the person receiving ministry from you. If your relationship with God is confrontational in any respect, do not minister until you have changed.

God answers prayer. Pray daily for ability to receive more of His love, ability to be a channel of His love to others and for guidance from and obedience to the leading of the Holy Spirit.

PRAYER AND WORSHIP

One must continually prepare to be used in ministry. Following are suggestions and scripture references to help increase the "anointing" on your life and ministry. You may not always feel the anointing, but it is with you and will increase if you ask.

Wait on the Lord in prayer.

> **PSALM 62:5**
> MY SOUL, WAIT SILENTLY FOR GOD ALONE; FOR MY EXPECTATION IS FROM HIM.
>
> **HOSEA 12:6**
> WAIT ON YOUR GOD CONTINUALLY.
>
> **ISAIAH 40:31 KJV**
> THEY THAT WAIT UPON THE LORD SHALL RENEW THEIR STRENGTH.

Ask the Holy Spirit to search your heart regularly.

> **PSALM 139: 23-24 KJV**
> SEARCH ME O GOD, AND KNOW MY HEART. TRY ME AND KNOW MY THOUGHTS. AND SEE IF THERE BE ANY WICKED WAY IN ME AND LEAD ME IN THE EVERLASTING WAY.
>
> **PSALM 51:10 KJV**
> CREATE IN ME A CLEAN HEART, O GOD, AND RENEW A RIGHT SPIRIT WITHIN ME.
>
> **PSALM 24:3-4 NIV**
> WHO MAY ASCEND THE HILL OF THE LORD? WHO MAY STAND IN HIS HOLY PLACE? HE

WHO HAS CLEAN HANDS AND A PURE HEART, WHO DOES NOT LIFT UP HIS SOUL TO AN IDOL OR SWEAR BY WHAT IS FALSE.

1 THESSALONIANS 5:19 (AMPLIFIED BIBLE)
DO NOTHING TO QUENCH (SUPPRESS OR SUBDUE) THE SPIRIT BY VIOLATING THE BIBLICAL PRINCIPLE OR YOUR CONSCIENCE.

EPHESIANS 5:18 (AMPLIFIED BIBLE)
AVAIL YOURSELF OF THE PRESENCE OF GOD AND KEEP RECEIVING MORE OF THE ANOINTING. "BUT EVER BE FILLED AND STIMULATED WITH THE HOLY SPIRIT."

EPHESIANS 4:23 (AMPLIFIED BIBLE)
RENEW YOUR MIND (HAVE A FRESH ATTITUDE) IN THE WORD. "BE CONSTANTLY RE- NEWED IN THE SPIRIT OF YOUR MIND."

Enter wholeheartedly into worship. Focus on Jesus and not on yourself.

PSALM 29:2
WORSHIP THE LORD IN THE BEAUTY OF HOLINESS.

PHILLIPPIANS 3:3
FOR WE ARE THE CIRCUMCISION, WHO WORSHIP GOD IN THE SPIRIT, REJOICE IN CHRIST JESUS, AND HAVE NO CONFIDENCE IN THE FLESH.

2 CORINTHIANS 10:5 KJV
CASTING DOWN IMAGINATIONS, AND EVERY HIGH THING THAT EXALTETH ITSELF AGAINST THE KNOWLEDGE OF GOD, AND BRINGING INTO CAPTIVITY EVERY THOUGHT TO THE OBEDIENCE OF CHRIST.

Receive prayer from others.

EPHESIANS 6:19 (NIV)
PRAY ALSO FOR ME, THAT WHENEVER I OPEN MY MOUTH, WORDS MAY BE GIVEN ME SO THAT I WILL FEARLESSLY MAKE KNOWN THE MYSTERY OF THE GOSPEL.

2 TIMOTHY 1:6
STIR UP* THE GIFT OF GOD WHICH IS IN YOU THROUGH THE LAYING ON OF MY HANDS. (*FAN THE FLAME OF, AND KEEP BURNING -AMPLIFIED BIBLE.)

Beware of being jealous of someone who seems more anointed than you are or of someone people wish to receive prayer from and line up for.

SPIRITUAL ATTACK

When you enlist for service to pray for others in specific ways, you are actively engaging in spiritual warfare. You are becoming a "freedom fighter" to help liberate the lost, the sick and the oppressed. The enemy does not take this invasion of his "turf" without retaliation. Do not be surprised at some form of counterattack.

Therefore, be on guard. Learn to rest in God when under attack. Rejoice in His care and His ability to protect you. Let the battle be the Lord's. Rest and peace are weapons designed to keep your heart (emotions) and your mind (the main battleground) in Christ Jesus (See Phillipians 4:6-7).

If you start experiencing sickness, difficulty at work, difficulty at home, or depression, for example, you do not have to endure it alone. Call a prayer partner you trust and get prayer. We are in this together!

SOME GENERAL SUGGESTIONS ON HOW TO PRAY

STYLE

Churches, conference leaders and individuals may have different styles of prayer during ministry time. Your prayer technique and personality will be different from others'. While you do not need to imitate another person's style, the following are some general guidelines that have proven safe and effective.

LOVE; COMFORT; EXHORT!

Remember that your two main guidelines are first, to show love, and second, to "comfort, exhort, and encourage." Apply this principle to the wording of your prayers. For example, if a person requests prayer for more trust in the Lord, it is better to pray, "Father, please increase my brother's faith" as opposed to "Father, deal with this evil heart of unbelief." Love and acceptance are key.

TAKE TIME TO MINISTER

Do not rush the work of the Holy Spirit. If someone falls down, ministry may continue as you pray over the person. Or you may be led to leave him alone with the Holy Spirit. If you speak to him, when preparing to leave, encourage the individual to remain on the floor and continue receiving. It is very common for people to get up too quickly and miss some of what God has for them.

USE DISCRETION

Do not minister to someone who does not want to be prayed for or does not ask for ministry. Allow God to work in the person's heart and draw that person to Himself in His time.

When under the influence of the Holy Spirit, people may reveal issues of a very personal nature. As a minister of healing, hold such disclosures with the utmost confidence.

When praying with someone concerning a sensitive matter, pray quietly so no one overhears you.

WAIT ON THE LORD

Do not "force" the work of the Spirit. If the person you are praying for is not in agreement, stop and change directions. If the Holy Spirit is specifically addressing something with the individual, let Him continue to deal with it, not you.

ASSESS RESPONSE

When praying for an individual, pay close attention to what the Spirit is doing. Pray with your eyes open. Watching the person's response to the Holy Spirit can assist you in cooperating with what God is doing in the person's heart. For example, if a person is trembling, you may want to continue the prayer you were praying when the trembling began. Or, if a person is weeping before the Lord, do not pray, "Lord, fill his mouth with laughter."

PRAY BIBLICAL PRAYERS

You will seldom err if you pray Biblical prayers such as:

"Come, Holy Spirit."

To receive the baptism of the Holy Spirit.

"More." ("How much more will the Father give the Holy Spirit to those who ask.")

A deeper revelation of the Father's love in Christ.

Anointing for service and/or a release of the gifts and calling.

Righteousness, peace, and joy.

A greater release of the kingdom of God.

For a spirit of love, or of peace, etc., to be on the person.

"SEE" SPIRITUALLY

Pray with your physical and spiritual eyes open. Do what you see the Father doing. If you receive insights or "words of knowledge," pray Biblical prayers related to those words. However, submit anything other than prayer for edification, exhortation, or comfort to a ministry team supervisor or pastor. Also, do not minister prophetic words to anyone high school age or younger without a parent or pastor present.

AVOID DISTRACTING ACTIONS

Use discretion with loud or intense prayer. In certain circumstances, it may distract the prayer recipient from what the Holy Spirit is trying to accomplish. Also, it can distract others being ministered to nearby. You may pray in the Spirit (tongues) quietly, but be sure that the individual receives prayer in English to edify and strengthen him or her.

AVOID THE FOLLOWING

Drawing attention to yourself by yelling, pushing, or waving your arms around.

Bumping people or touching them in such a way that will distract from the Holy Spirit's work. Allow God to touch them.

Forcing a tissue into someone's hands. Be discerning and sensitive.

Asking a lot of questions. You are a facilitator for the Holy Spirit, not a counselor. He will minister to them.

Projecting what God has been doing with you onto the person requesting prayer. For example, if you have been laughing, don't pressure him to laugh. Find out what God is doing for him and bless it.

Conversing near people receiving ministry.

TEST YOUR IMPRESSIONS

When in doubt, stop and ask. If you feel a particular impression in your spirit, but want to make sure that it is from the Lord, ask the person if your impression makes sense or means anything to him or her. If the person says yes, then faith increases for the both of you. If the person says no, you have proven yourself prudent.

EMPHASIZE THE POSITIVE

Do not minister any directional or correctional prophecy. Instead, minister positive words such as encouragement, prayer to receive the baptism of the Holy Spirit and healing strength.

WHEN TO STOP PRAYING

An important factor is how many people want prayer compared with the size of the ministry team. The first hour is usually the most demanding. If there are many people waiting for you to pray for them, it is usually wise to allow five or six minutes per person, especially if there does not seem to be much evidence of the moving of the Holy Spirit (such as tears, trembling, or prayer direction). You might suggest that the person continue to soak and tell him that you will come back a little later.

However, when the Holy Spirit is moving strongly, continue praying with the person, even if others are waiting. Always take your time and be patient. The goal is quality, not quantity.

If no one is waiting for you, you might continue to pray for the person even if there is no strong manifestation of the Holy Spirit working.

If you say you will come back and pray more for someone, be sure to do it.

If the person you are praying for falls, continue praying for him until the Holy Spirit releases you. God continues working even when the person is down on the floor. Sometimes His work is noticeable. Other times, it is quiet and inward. Encouraging the person to get up too quickly seems to work against what the Lord wants to do.

HELPING THOSE WHO HAVE DIFFICULTY RECEIVING

For some people, coming forward for prayer is difficult. In fact, some may have come to an altar only once or twice their entire lives. It is natural for them to feel apprehension and uncertainty. These feelings may then become compounded if they do not quickly "sense" the moving of the Holy Spirit during prayer. This can result in a person leaving the altar confused and discouraged instead of spiritually refreshed. Try to put such persons at ease. Be relaxed yourself. It is appropriate to engage the person in quiet conversation of a friendly nature.

You might ask if he or she has ever received renewal prayer before and how it went. This gives you an opportunity to address his or her fears.

As to receiving prayer, the following suggestions may be helpful for those who are ill at ease or slower to receive.

If after a few minutes of prayer, you either sense or observe that the person is not receiving anything, feel free to inquire: "Is the Lord speaking to you?" or "Do you sense the Holy Spirit doing anything?" If not, perhaps he or she needs more instruction and encouragement.

You may be able to say something encouraging or which might alleviate his fears. Some possible examples:

> Encourage the prayee to relax and receive. Suggest that he or she not pray, not aloud or even silently, or in tongues, but just to put his mind in neutral and receive. "We all spend much of our lives working and giving out; this is a time just to receive. You can pray all the way home!"

> "It's a good idea just to soak. Think of yourself as a dry sponge and the Holy Spirit as rain. Just remain in His presence during the worship and prayer time and let Him begin to saturate you."

> "Try to put the manifestations out of your mind. This is simply about getting closer to the Lord and having your spirit refreshed. If you feel like falling, that's fine; someone is behind you to catch you. But it isn't necessary. Just open your spirit to the Holy Spirit and see what happens."

> If necessary, calm the person's fear of loss of control by helping him or her know what to expect. "Your mind will always remain clear. Even if the Holy Spirit moves in some unusual way, you can stop the process anytime you want to."

> "Go with the flow. If you feel an inclination to cry, laugh, smile or even tremble, go with it. You're in a very safe place here."

> Assure the person that there is nothing wrong with him or her. It's very natural for the person to think, "Everyone else is getting blessed and there must be something wrong with me." That's probably not true. "Just be patient with yourself and the Lord. If you are really concerned that there is an obstacle in your life, just ask the Lord -- He'll tell you what it is."

> Help the person deal with rationalization tendencies, fears or loss of control. "Just experience it. Don't try to analyze it. It is something like worshipping God. There isn't really a rational explanation."

> Some people fear falling. If the person has back problems, is pregnant, is elderly, is very heavy or frail, or fears falling, you may want to ask if he or she would like to sit down to receive prayer. If he wishes to stand, get enough help to make sure he can be assisted down carefully.

> Encourage the person to focus on the Lord, and not on falling. "Give the Holy Spirit permission to do what He wants to do."

> "It's always acceptable to receive more prayer. It's not selfish to want more of God. In fact, it's a great sign of spiritual health. Receive prayer whenever possible."

The important thing is, don't force ministry. If the Spirit is not doing something, you may need to remember to relax and realize that there will be other opportunities.

PRAYERS OF BLESSING

The source of all blessing is God. In His goodness, He allows us, His children, to communicate His blessings by our words and deeds. The difference between genuine blessing and more common well-wishing is that one originates with God and the other with man. For words of blessing to have any authority or power, they must align with scripture and the purpose of God in the recipient's life.

The key element in praying a blessing on others is to know that what you are praying represents God's heart and desire for that person.

Begin by praying with an open ear to God. Expect Him to reveal something of His purpose for the person's life. He may do this through a specific scripture, word picture, spiritual impression or by quickening to your memory something you already know about the person.

Review the paragraph above on praying Biblical prayers.

A SAMPLE PRAYER

The following is a sample prayer in procedural form that begins with general blessing while waiting on the Lord and continues to more specific blessing as He reveals more specific areas of need.

Begin with a simple statement:

"I bless you (or use the person's name) in the name of Jesus Christ."

Continue with general prayers of blessing from scripture; for example:

"Lord, I pray You will pour out Your blessings upon (person's name) and heal his (or her) infirmities, heal any wounds or scars in his heart, bless his family, bless him with financial provision and protect him from the evil one."

Speak prayers of specific blessings such as:

"Father, bless (person's name) by restoring the broken relationship he (or she) has with his (or her) teen-age daughter. Break down the walls of rebellion and estrangement that have been built up between them. Give each of them a great love for the other. Help them to respect each other, and to be comfortable with each other..."

"Father, touch him with Your love. Reveal to him how precious he is in Your sight. Lift away from him all his fears and anxieties about You. Let Your blessings flow over him."

MINISTRY TO PEOPLE IN A GROUP

There may be occasions, as at an altar call for a purpose named by the speaker, when you will minister to individuals who are part of a large group. The following suggestions apply to how you might select whom to pray for and some thoughts about your ministry:

ASSESSING READINESS

Begin with those who appear to be open to the Holy Spirit. For example, someone whose eyes are closed and who appears to be lost in worship is probably more ready for the Holy Spirit's work than someone whose hands are in his pockets and whose eyes are wandering. This way, you start on an encouraging note. Those who are a bit distracted then have a few minutes to "soak" (time in God's presence).

ADMINISTERING PROTECTION

Be aware of people who have fallen down. Protect them from being bumped, stepped on or having someone else fall on them.

Be sensitive to cover a person if dignity requires it. Gently adjust his posture if needed.

REFERENCE THE MESSAGE

At a meeting, if there is a specific altar call, make sure to address the subject of the altar call or of the speaker's message in your prayer. It was the Holy Spirit who caused the individual to respond to the altar call in the first place. Our responsibility is to cooperate with Him.

Pray in accordance with the altar call. If it is for healing, find out what healing is needed and pray for that. If it is for rededication, encourage the person to rededicate his life now, while you listen. If it is for impartation, pray for impartation of the gift the speaker has called people to receive. If the call is for release of bondages, pray for deliverance from the bondages the speaker mentioned, or that the person mentions to you. In any case of deliverance, if there are manifestations, the spirit should be quieted and the person should be taken to a quiet place for extended ministry.

If there is no clear indication of the nature of the altar call, as often occurs in ministry after a church service for example, ask the person for his or her prayer request. If you are in doubt about his salvation, ask if he is saved and if not. See if you can lead him to Jesus.

LOVE, LOVE, LOVE!

If you are a channel for the love of God, the people you pray for will receive a genuine ministry and blessing, whether or not they receive the other things you may pray for. God is love. If we are ministering in His Spirit, we will impart something of His love to those we pray for.

Be a blessing!

Chapter 3
SOZO

"SOZO"

The word "sozo" is used more than 110 times in the New Testament. It is a Greek verb or action word meaning to be saved or rescued out from under Satan's power and restored into the wholeness of God's order and well-being. It is used to mean *saved* in the sense of being saved from eternal punishment for sin. It is used to mean to be *healed* of disease. It is used to mean to be *delivered* from demonic oppression. In fact, it can mean all three of these at the same time. It is also used as the verb when someone is raised from the dead. To be "sozo," is to be saved completely.

SALVATION

Peter, preaching to the elders and rulers of Jerusalem said:

> **ACTS 4:12 (NIV)**
> SALVATION IS FOUND IN NO ONE ELSE, FOR THERE IS NO OTHER NAME UNDER HEAVEN GIVEN TO MEN BY WHICH WE MUST BE (SOZO) SAVED.

Paul wrote to the Christians at Rome:

> **ROMANS 10:9 (NIV)**
> IF YOU CONFESS WITH YOUR MOUTH, "JESUS IS LORD", AND BELIEVE IN YOUR HEART THAT GOD RAISED HIM FROM THE DEAD, YOU WILL BE (SOZO) SAVED.

And to the church at Ephesus:

> **EPHESIANS 2:8 (NIV)**
> FOR IT IS BY GRACE YOU HAVE BEEN (SOZO) SAVED, THROUGH FAITH, AND THIS NOT FROM YOURSELVES, IT IS THE GIFT OF GOD...

HEALING

MATTHEW 9:22 (NIV)
JESUS TURNED AND SAW HER. TAKE HEART, DAUGHTER," HE SAID. "YOUR FAITH HAS (SOZO) HEALED YOU." AND THE WOMAN WAS (SOZO) HEALED FROM THAT MOMENT.

MARK 6:56 (NIV)
AND EVERYWHERE HE WENT, INTO VILLAGES, TOWNS OR COUNTRYSIDE, THEY PLACED THE SICK IN THE MARKET PLACES. THEY BEGGED HIM TO LET THEM TOUCH EVEN THE EDGE OF HIS CLOAK, AND ALL WHO TOUCHED HIM WERE (SOZO) HEALED.

MARK 10:52 (NIV)
"GO," SAID JESUS. "YOUR FAITH HAS (SOZO) HEALED YOU." IMMEDIATELY HE RECEIVED HIS SIGHT AND FOLLOWED JESUS ALONG THE ROAD.

DELIVERANCE

LUKE 8:36 (NIV)
THOSE WHO HAD SEEN IT TOLD THE PEOPLE HOW THE DEMON-POSSESSED MAN HAD BEEN (SOZO) CURED.

2 TIMOTHY 4:18 (NIV)
THE LORD WILL (SOZO) RESCUE ME FROM EVERY EVIL ATTACK AND WILL BRING ME SAFELY TO HIS HEAVENLY KINGDOM. TO HIM BE GLORY FOR EVER AND EVER. AMEN.

JUDE 1:5 (NIV)
THOUGH YOU ALREADY KNOW ALL THIS, I WANT TO REMIND YOU THAT THE LORD (SOZO) DELIVERED HIS PEOPLE OUT OF EGYPT, BUT LATER DESTROYED THOSE WHO DID NOT BELIEVE.

SALVATION, HEALING, AND DELIVERANCE!

LUKE 19:9-10 (NIV)
JESUS SAID, "FOR THE SON OF MAN CAME TO SEEK AND TO SAVE (SOZO) WHAT WAS LOST."

JOHN 20:21 (NIV)
"PEACE BE WITH YOU! AS THE FATHER HAS SENT ME, I AM SENDING YOU."

When you minister salvation, healing or deliverance to a needy person, you have rescued him from the power of Satan in that area. You have weakened Satan's kingdom and strengthened the kingdom of God.

Chapter 4
SALVATION

CHANGE
SOME DEFINITIONS

"Sinner" means a person who has broken one or more of God's laws. This includes everyone.

"Death," "darkness," "hell," "perish" and similar words refer to the destiny of unsaved persons after death. It is what all sinners deserve (See Romans 3:23 and Romans 6:23).

"Heaven," "everlasting life," "eternal life" and similar words refer to the destiny of saved persons after death. It is the eternal life provided by God for those who believe in Jesus.

"The cross" means the cross on which Jesus was crucified to pay the penalty for our sins. We no longer need to pay the penalty for sins ourselves.

"Christian" and "believer" mean a person who believes that Jesus died on the cross to save him from his sins, that He was raised from the dead and who has decided to follow Jesus as the Lord of his life.

"Unbeliever" refers to someone who has not trusted that Jesus died on the cross to save him from his sins and has not received Jesus as the Lord of his life.

"Converted" means changed from an unbeliever in Jesus to a believer in Jesus.

To "repent" means to be convinced that sin is wrong and decided to turn away from sin. It means to re-think about the issues of life.

To be "saved" means to become a believer, to be rescued from the destiny of death and darkness to the destiny of heaven.

"Salvation" refers to the process or result of being "converted" or "saved". This process usually includes the following steps:

> to believe that Jesus is the Son of God,
>
> to believe that Jesus died on the cross to take the punishment for sin that we deserve, and thus to save us from our sins,
>
> to repent of our sins, and
>
> to confess Jesus as the Lord of our life.

"Son of Man" is a title Jesus often used to refer to Himself.

"The Atonement" refers to Jesus' work to bring sinners who are estranged from God by their sin into a right relationship with God. As such, it generally refers to the punishment He suffered in place of the punishment men deserve for their sin: His arrest, His suffering under Pilate, His death on the cross.

CONVERSION IS A RENEWING EXPERIENCE

"They who are truly converted are new men, new creatures; new, not only within, but without... they have new hearts, new eyes, new ears, new tongues, new hands, new feet."

Jonathan Edwards

2 CORINTHIANS 5:17 (NIV)
THEREFORE, IF ANYONE IS IN CHRIST, HE IS A NEW CREATION; OLD THINGS HAVE PASSED AWAY; BEHOLD, ALL THINGS HAVE BECOME NEW.

Spiritual change – conversion – requires four things:

> Conviction of sin, provided by the Holy Spirit
>
> Repentance or turning away from sin. The desire to repent is also provided by the Holy Spirit. It is a gift (See Acts 10:45).
>
> Asking forgiveness for one's sins
>
> A decision to receive Jesus as the Lord of one's life. The decision to receive Jesus as Lord requires the enabling grace of the Holy Spirit

WE ARE CHANGED BY GRACE

Heaven is a free gift – it cannot be earned. It is never deserved. Salvation is a free gift. It cannot be earned. It is never deserved.

The following are some Biblical truths about grace:

Man is a sinner.

> **ROMANS 3:23 (NIV)**
> FOR ALL HAVE SINNED AND FALL SHORT OF THE GLORY OF GOD.
>
> **ISAIAH 53:6 (NIV)**
> WE ALL, LIKE SHEEP, HAVE GONE ASTRAY, EACH OF US HAS TURNED TO HIS OWN WAY;
> AND THE LORD HAS LAID ON HIM THE INIQUITY OF US ALL.

The consequence of sin is death.

> **ROMANS 6:23 (NIV)**
> FOR THE WAGES OF SIN IS DEATH...

Man cannot save himself.

> **ROMANS 6:23 (NIV)**
> FOR THE WAGES OF SIN IS DEATH, BUT THE GIFT OF GOD IS ETERNAL LIFE IN CHRIST
> JESUS OUR LORD.
>
> **EPHISEANS 2:8-9 (NIV)**
> FOR IT IS BY GRACE YOU HAVE BEEN SAVED, THROUGH FAITH - AND THIS NOT FROM
> YOURSELVES, IT IS THE GIFT OF GOD - NOT BY WORKS, SO THAT NO ONE CAN BOAST.

Jesus is the Son of God, a member of the Triune God.

> **JOHN 1:1 (NIV)**
> IN THE BEGINNING WAS THE WORD, AND THE WORD WAS WITH GOD, AND THE WORD
> WAS GOD.
>
> **JOHN 1:14 (NIV)**
> THE WORD BECAME FLESH AND MADE HIS DWELLING AMONG US. WE HAVE SEEN HIS
> GLORY, THE GLORY OF THE ONE AND ONLY, WHO CAME FROM THE FATHER, FULL OF
> GRACE AND TRUTH.

Jesus came to earth to save us from the consequences of our sin.

> **JOHN 3:16**
> FOR GOD SO LOVED THE WORLD THAT HE GAVE HIS ONLY BEGOTTEN SON, THAT WHO-
> EVER BELIEVES IN HIM SHOULD NOT PERISH, BUT HAVE EVERLASTING LIFE.
>
> **1 TIMOTHY 1:15**
> THIS IS A FAITHFUL SAYING AND WORTHY OF ALL ACCEPTANCE, THAT CHRIST JESUS
> CAME INTO THE WORLD TO SAVE SINNERS...FOR THE SON OF MAN HAS COME TO SEEK
> AND TO SAVE THAT WHICH WAS LOST. (LUKE 19:10.)

> **LUKE 19:10**
> FOR THE SON OF MAN HAS COME TO SEEK AND TO SAVE THAT WHICH WAS LOST.

Jesus paid the penalty for our sins. On the cross, God treated Jesus as if He had committed our sins.

> **1 PETER 2:24**
> ...WHO HIMSELF BORE OUR SINS IN HIS OWN BODY ON THE TREE, THAT WE, HAVING DIED TO SINS, MIGHT LIVE FOR RIGHTEOUSNESS.

If we wish to know what God thinks of our disobedience and sin, consider what the cross meant for Jesus.

> **LUKE 22:41-44 (NIV)**
> AND HE WITHDREW FROM THEM ABOUT A STONE'S THROW, AND KNELT DOWN AND PRAYED, SAYING, "FATHER, IF IT IS YOUR WILL, REMOVE THIS CUP FROM ME, NEVERTHELESS NOT MY WILL, BUT YOURS, BE DONE." THEN AN ANGEL APPEARED TO HIM FROM HEAVEN, STRENGTHENING HIM. AND BEING IN AGONY, HE PRAYED MORE EARNESTLY. AND HIS SWEAT BECAME LIKE GREAT DROPS OF BLOOD FALLING DOWN TO THE GROUND.

This will give us a small idea of the immeasurable blessing of salvation.

> **2 PETER 3:9**
> THE LORD IS... NOT WILLING THAT ANY SHOULD PERISH BUT THAT ALL SHOULD COME TO REPENTANCE.

We are saved only by faith in Jesus Christ. Christ paid for our sins and purchased a place in heaven for us which He offers as a gift. This alone is our salvation. Faith in Christ is not mere intellectual assent. It is trusting in Him alone for salvation and purposing in our heart to make Him Lord of our life.

> **EPHESIANS 2:8 (NIV)**
> FOR IT IS BY GRACE YOU HAVE BEEN SAVED, THROUGH FAITH...
>
> **ROMANS 10:9 (NIV)**
> ...IF YOU CONFESS WITH YOUR MOUTH "JESUS IS LORD", AND BELIEVE IN YOUR HEART THAT GOD RAISED HIM FROM THE DEAD, YOU WILL BE SAVED.
>
> **ACTS 4:12**
> NOR IS THERE SALVATION IN ANY OTHER, FOR THERE IS NO OTHER NAME UNDER HEAVEN GIVEN AMONG MEN BY WHICH WE MUST BE SAVED.

A SALVATION MINISTRY MODEL

This salvation ministry model is a four-step process:

1. PREPARATION

The one ministering salvation should talk with the person seeking salvation to make sure that the person understands his condition and is making a voluntary decision to repent and turn to the Lord for salvation and lordship. A review of the points mentioned above and reference to the appropriate scriptures may be helpful. The one ministering should be confident that:

The person seeking salvation is under the conviction of the Holy Spirit and understands that he or she is a sinner.

He understands the guilt of sin and that because of his sin, he deserves eternal death or hell.

He wants to be saved.

He understands that Jesus was a sinless man. He was the Son of God. Jesus paid the penalty that he would otherwise have had to pay. Only Jesus could pay this penalty because only Jesus was without sin.

He understands that only trusting in Jesus can ensure salvation. (That is, salvation cannot be earned by doing more good things than bad things in this life.) He wants to live under the authority – under the lordship – of Jesus Christ from now on.

There are several things the minister might mention to the seeker.

Remind him that God listens to his heart.

> **JEREMIAH 29:13 (NIV)**
> YOU WILL SEEK ME AND FIND ME WHEN YOU SEEK ME WITH ALL YOUR HEART.

Remind the person that God is present right now.

> **MATTHEW 18:20 (NIV)**
> FOR WHERE TWO OR THREE COME TOGETHER IN MY NAME, THERE AM I WITH THEM.

Remind him that God loves him and wants him to be saved.

> **JOHN 3:16**
> FOR GOD SO LOVED THE WORLD ...
>
> **2 PETER 3:9**
> THE LORD IS ... NOT WILLING THAT ANY SHOULD PERISH, BUT THAT ALL SHOULD COME TO REPENTANCE.

Remind him that the Holy Spirit will help him.

Tell him that the Christian life is not necessarily easy, but that it offers peace.

Suggest a simple prayer for the person to repeat after you. Such a prayer might be:

> "Lord Jesus, I want you to come in and take over my life right now. I am a sinner. I have been trusting in myself and my own good works to get me to heaven. But now I place my trust in You. I believe that You are God and that You paid the price for all the punishment that I deserve, because of what I have done. I ask You to forgive me for the bad things that I have done and wanted to do."

2. CONFESSION AND REPENTANCE

Ask the person to make specific confession of his sins, indicating his repentance for each one and asking God for His forgiveness for each one.

At this point, ask the person to confess to God audibly and in your presence, each separate specific sin the Holy Spirit brings to his mind. Such confession requires the person to be honest with himself and brings each sin into the light. The person should tell God that he repents of each sin mentioned and intends in his heart to turn away from it. Then he should ask God's forgiveness for each of these sins.

The more specific this confession is the better. It should not be hurried. Give the Holy Spirit time to speak to the seeker's mind.

Some Ways the Person Might Pray

> "Dear God, I confess that I have sinned against you by the resentment and anger and bitterness I have felt against my father. I repent of my resentment and anger and bitterness toward him, and turn away from them. I intend in my heart to love him from now on as You give me grace to do that. Please forgive me for these sins."
>
> "God, I confess that I have rebelled against my parents and against You. I repent of my rebellion. I intend to honor my parents. Please forgive me for my rebellion."
>
> "Dear God, I confess that I have abused my body with marihuana, speed, crack and alcohol. I repent of taking these things into my body, and I turn my back on all drugs and alcohol. I intend to have nothing to do with them any more. Please forgive me for abusing my body with these drugs."
>
> "Dear God, I confess that I have sinned against your word by reading horoscopes and seeing fortune tellers. I repent of having read horoscopes and seeing fortune tellers. I intend never to do those things again. Please forgive me for these sins."
>
> "Dear God, I confess that I have shared my body outside of marriage with Tom and Harry and Warren (naming each person by first name). I realize that each one of these relationships was sinful. I repent of these sins, and I purpose in my heart to turn away from all fornication from now on. Please forgive me for each time I have sinned with these people."

Allow a few minutes of silence to let the Holy Spirit bring to the person's mind any other sins He wants to bring up for confession and repentance.

Some Suggestions About Hearing Confession

Don't be shocked at anything you hear.

Remember that all confession is absolutely confidential. The only exceptions are if the person making confession asks you to discuss something with someone else or if disclosure is legally required (such as child molestation, rape or murder).

Remember that specific confession is more helpful than general confession.

Don't engage in unguided flesh hunts. Guidance in repentance is the work of the Holy Spirit. Simply encourage him to confess what the Holy Spirit lays on his heart. Tell him that the Holy Spirit may bring other sins to his mind later, and he should confess, repent and ask forgiveness for them then.

Be careful that you do not get drawn into any sin confessed to you.

> **GALATIONS 6:1 (NIV)**
> BROTHERS, IF SOMEONE IS CAUGHT IN A SIN, YOU WHO ARE SPIRITUAL SHOULD RE-STORE HIM GENTLY. BUT WATCH YOURSELF, OR YOU ALSO MAY BE TEMPTED.

Don't interrupt the confession to give advice or teaching. The important thing at such a time is for the person you are helping to do genuine business with God, as completely as the Holy Spirit leads him. Advice or teaching can stop the confession process. There will be time for advice or teaching later

3. COMMITMENT

After the person has made as complete a confession and repentance as the Holy Spirit seems to lead in, you can conclude the prayer time by asking him or her to receive Jesus as Lord. You might suggest that he pray:

> "Jesus, I ask You now to come and take control of my life. I will do whatever You tell me to do. Help me to turn from my sins and to follow You. I accept Your free gift of eternal life. I know I am not worthy of it, but I thank You for it. Please fill me with the Holy Spirit now and give me grace so that I can keep these promises. Amen."

> **LUKE 11:13 (NIV)**
> IF YOU THEN, THOUGH YOU ARE EVIL, KNOW HOW TO GIVE GOOD GIFTS TO YOUR CHIL-DREN, HOW MUCH MORE WILL YOUR FATHER IN HEAVEN GIVE THE HOLY SPIRIT TO THOSE WHO ASK HIM!

4. THANKSGIVING

Thank God for the seeker's confession and ask the Holy Spirit to fill him.

Then you lay your hands on the person's head. Thank God for his or her confession and repentance and pray for the person to be filled with the Holy Spirit.

The seeker will probably want to thank God for himself. He should be encouraged to do this. Occasionally the seeker may sink to the floor when you pray for him. In that case, if he can hear you, you should encourage him to rest there for a time until the Holy Spirit moves him to get up.

> **1 JOHN 1:9 (NIV)**
> IF WE CONFESS OUR SINS, HE IS FAITHFUL AND JUST AND WILL FORGIVE US OUR SINS AND PURIFY US FROM ALL UNRIGHTEOUSNESS.

> **JOHN 20:23 (NIV)**
> IF YOU FORGIVE ANYONE HIS SINS, THEY ARE FORGIVEN; IF YOU DO NOT FORGIVE THEM, THEY ARE NOT FORGIVEN.
>
> **2 CORINTHIANS 2:10-11 (NIV)**
> IF YOU FORGIVE ANYONE, I ALSO FORGIVE HIM. AND WHAT I HAVE FORGIVEN - IF THERE WAS ANYTHING TO FORGIVE - I HAVE FORGIVEN IN THE SIGHT OF CHRIST FOR YOUR SAKE, IN ORDER THAT SATAN MIGHT NOT OUTWIT US ... FOR WE ARE NOT UNAWARE OF HIS SCHEMES.

THE AUTHORITY TO FORGIVE

Just as Jesus allows us to participate in the ministries of salvation, healing and deliverance, so too He allows us to participate in the ministry of forgiveness.

> **JOHN 6:47**
> "MOST ASSUREDLY, I SAY TO YOU, HE WHO BELIEVES IN ME HAS EVERLASTING LIFE."

You may look the prayee in the eye and say to him or her: "In the name of Jesus, you are forgiven."

SOME NOTES

Encourage the person not to leave until you both know that he or she really is saved!

Pray for healing, if needed.

Ask the seeker to read John 6:47.

Give him the follow-up materials your church uses.

Tell him to get rid of any paraphernalia he may have that is associated with the sins he has confessed, such as drugs, needles, pornographic magazines, horoscopes, New Age books, tokens, Masonic jewelry or symbols, etc. Such items should not be given away to someone else, they should be destroyed.

Pray unhurriedly for any other needs you see that he has and for God's blessings over him.

Tell him that confession, repentance and asking forgiveness need to become his lifestyle.

Tell him that confession and forgiveness probably will not be complete at the time of conversion. The Holy Spirit will take the seeker as far as the seeker can go at this time. He will recall other sins that need to be confessed, repented of, and forgiveness asked. He should be encouraged to follow through with respect to these sins as he is reminded of them by the Holy Spirit. It is best if this is done audibly with a trusted friend.

The seeker will also remember additional things done or said that caused him hurt or distress – things he did not remember at the time of conversion. He will often need to forgive a particular person more than once. He may need to forgive the same person for the same deed, more than once. You may need to mention this so such happenings will not be a source of discouragement to him.

Also, the seeker will be reminded by the Holy Spirit of additional misdeeds for which he needs to ask forgiveness. That he did not remember at the time of his original confession. He will need to confess, repent and ask forgiveness of these misdeeds. Such happenings are normal. The seeker should not be discouraged because of them. You may want to mention this to him.

The Holy Spirit may move you to keep in touch with the new believer. If He does, be sure to obey! It may save the seeker from backsliding.

Chapter 5
A BIBLICAL BASIS FOR HEALING THE SICK

SUMMARY

HEALING THE SICK IS A SIGNIFICANT SPIRITUAL MINISTRY

Healing the sick is a benefit of the Atonement by which hurting men are set free from physical bondage.

God releases the blessings of the Atonement through ministries of men.

Jesus regarded His healing of the sick:

> As proof that He was the awaited Messiah.
>
> As proof that He had authority on earth to forgive sins.
>
> As evidence to others that the kingdom of God was at hand.
>
> As an evidence of the love of God.
>
> As an evidence of the power of God.
>
> As one of the primary aids to evangelism by His disciples.

Healing the sick was a commission to Jesus' disciples when He was on earth.

Healing the sick is a commission to Jesus' disciples today.

A biblical basis for ministry to the sick is, at the same time and to the same extent, a biblical basis for the ministry of deliverance. Among the several reasons for this statement are the following:

Throughout the gospels, references to Jesus' ministry usually include both healing the sick and casting out demons. Most of the Lord's comments about either ministry seem to apply to both.

In several instances, the word "healing" or equivalent seems intended to include deliverance from demonic oppression. An example is Luke's comment about Jesus' ministry when

John's disciples came to Him. Luke says: "And that very hour He cured many people of their infirmities, afflictions, and evil spirits…" (Luke 7:21 NKJV). Another example is Luke's description of the ministry of the twelve disciples after being sent out by Jesus: "Then He called His twelve disciples together and gave them power and authority over all demons, and to cure diseases… So they departed and went through the towns, preaching the gospel and healing everywhere." (Luke 9:1-6 NKJV)

That the ministries of healing and deliverance are to be considered similarly is indicated in the commission to the disciples mentioned above and in the great commission of Jesus as set out in Mark 16: "And these signs will follow those who believe: In My name they will cast out demons … they will lay hands on the sick, and they will recover." (Mark 16:17-18 NKJV)

WHAT IS GOD'S PROVISION FOR "DIVINE" HEALING?

In our fallen world, all kinds of illnesses, injuries and emotional dysfunctions abound. Medical help benefits many. Although sometimes improvement from medical help is slow. Sometimes it is even ineffective. For some, medical help is not available or not desired. For these and other reasons, many people have an interest in seeking divine healing. What provision has God made for effective healing through prayer?

The answer is healing, like salvation, has been provided for in the Atonement[1].

It is familiar theology that Jesus, by giving His life on the cross, paid the price for our salvation. Jesus took on himself the penalty for our sins and that through faith in Him, we can be saved from punishment for our sins and moved from eternal death to eternal life.

It is perhaps somewhat less familiar theology that Jesus, in His Atonement, also paid the price

JOHN 3:16-17
FOR GOD SO LOVED THE WORLD THAT HE GAVE HIS ONLY BEGOTTEN SON, THAT WHOEVER BELIEVES IN HIM SHOULD NOT PERISH BUT HAVE EVERLASTING LIFE. FOR GOD DID NOT SEND HIS SON INTO THE WORLD TO CONDEMN THE WORLD, BUT THAT THE WORLD THROUGH HIM MIGHT BE SAVED.

JOHN 6:47
"MOST ASSUREDLY, I SAY TO YOU, HE WHO BELIEVES IN ME HAS EVERLASTING LIFE."

ROMANS 5:8 (NIV)
BUT GOD DEMONSTRATES HIS OWN LOVE FOR US IN THIS: WHILE WE WERE STILL SINNERS, CHRIST DIED FOR US.

1 CORINTHIANS 6:19-20 (NIV)
DO YOU NOT KNOW THAT YOUR BODY IS A TEMPLE OF THE HOLY SPIRIT WHO IS IN YOU, WHOM YOU HAVE RECEIVED FROM GOD? YOU ARE NOT YOUR OWN; YOU WERE BOUGHT AT A PRICE. THEREFORE HONOR GOD IN YOUR BODY.

[1]The word "Atonement" as used here means "'a making at one', … a process of bringing those who are estranged into a unity." The New Bible Dictionary, Eerdmans, 1962, p. 107. Here, it refers to Christ's suffering at the hands of Pilate, and his crucifixion.

for the healing of physical and emotional illness. Yet the scripture indicates that this is so. Isaiah prophesied:

> **ISAIAH 53:4-5 (NIV)**
> SURELY HE TOOK UP OUR INFIRMITIES (LITERALLY, "SICKNESSES"3) AND CARRIED OUR SORROWS (LITERALLY, "PAINS"4), YET WE CONSIDERED HIM STRICKEN BY GOD, SMITTEN BY HIM, AND AFFLICTED. BUT HE WAS PIERCED FOR OUR TRANSGRESSIONS, HE WAS CRUSHED FOR OUR INIQUITIES; THE PUNISHMENT THAT BROUGHT US PEACE WAS UPON HIM, AND BY HIS WOUNDS WE ARE HEALED.

Matthew quotes from this passage, saying:

> **MATTHEW 8:16-17 (NIV)**
> WHEN EVENING CAME, MANY WHO WERE DEMON-POSSESSED WERE BROUGHT TO HIM, AND HE DROVE OUT THE SPIRITS WITH A WORD AND HEALED ALL THE SICK. THIS WAS TO FULFILL WHAT WAS SPOKEN BY THE PROPHET ISAIAH: "HE TOOK UP OUR INFIRMITIES AND CARRIED OUR DISEASES."

Peter commented of the Lord's passion:

> **1 PETER 2:24**
> ... WHO HIMSELF BORE OUR SINS IN HIS OWN BODY ON THE TREE, THAT WE, HAVING DIED TO SINS, MIGHT LIVE FOR RIGHTEOUSNESS – BY WHOSE STRIPES YOU WERE HEALED.

In Christ's atonement, God has provided for many blessings for the world He loves. Jesus' death and resurrection was a complete triumph over Satan and his kingdom. The Atonement affords freedom from every bondage Satan can muster: freedom from bondage to sin; freedom from bondage to guilt and shame; freedom from bondage to demonic oppression, to any or all curses, to any or all satanic activity; freedom from bondage to sickness, disease and emotional illness.

However, the blessings of the Atonement are not automatic. As discussed more fully below, healings, like most of the blessings of the atonement, are usually released to people through the agency of others' prayers and actions. In the case of healings, this means praying for the sick.[2]

WHY DID JESUS HEAL THE SICK?

Beyond question, healing the sick was a central part of Jesus' ministry. When He referred to the prophecy about himself in Isaiah 61, He mentioned specifically healing the broken-hearted, deliverance to captives, recovery of sight to the blind and setting at liberty those who are oppressed (Luke 4:18). In the gospels, most references to His ministry state that, along with His teaching or preaching, He healed the sick and cast out demons.

[2]In the case of demonic oppression, of course, this means casting out demons.

Why did He make healing such a central part of His ministry? He did not say specifically, but several conclusions can be drawn from the scripture:

JESUS REGARDED HIS LIFE AND MINISTRY AS A FULFILLMENT OF PROPHECIES THAT HE WOULD HEAL THE SICK

Jesus knew that He had been sent by His Father on a mission to earth. He commented many times that His Father had "sent" Him. For example:

> **JOHN 5:36**
> "BUT I HAVE A GREATER WITNESS THAN JOHN'S; FOR THE WORKS WHICH THE FATHER HAS GIVEN ME TO FINISH - THE VERY WORKS THAT I DO - BEAR WITNESS OF ME, THAT THE FATHER HAS SENT ME."
>
> **JOHN 6:37-38**
> "ALL THAT THE FATHER GIVES ME WILL COME TO ME, AND THE ONE WHO COMES TO ME I WILL BY NO MEANS CAST OUT. FOR I HAVE COME DOWN FROM HEAVEN, NOT TO DO MY OWN WILL, BUT THE WILL OF HIM WHO SENT ME."
>
> **JOHN 7:33**
> "I SHALL BE WITH YOU A LITTLE WHILE LONGER, AND THEN I GO TO HIM WHO SENT ME."

Nearly a dozen times, as in John 6:38 and 7:33 set out above, Jesus referred to His Father as "him that sent me." That He was a "sent one" had been earlier expressed by the prophet Isaiah whom Jesus quoted in Nazareth when He said He was fulfilling the prophecy of Isaiah 61:1-2.

> **LUKE 4:18-19, 21**
> "THE SPIRIT OF THE LORD IS UPON ME, BECAUSE HE HAS ANOINTED ME TO PREACH THE GOSPEL TO THE POOR. HE HAS SENT ME TO HEAL THE BROKENHEARTED, TO PREACH DELIVERANCE TO THE CAPTIVES AND RECOVERY OF SIGHT TO THE BLIND, TO SET AT LIBERTY THOSE WHO ARE OPPRESSED, TO PREACH THE ACCEPTABLE YEAR OF THE LORD." AND THEN HE SAID: "TODAY THIS SCRIPTURE IS FULFILLED IN YOUR HEARING."

Jesus' knowledge that He was fulfilling prophecy was expressed in a comment recorded in Matthew:

As noted above in John 7:33, Jesus knew that when His mission on earth was finished, He would return to His Father in heaven.

> **MATTHEW 5:17-18**
> "DO NOT THINK THAT I CAME TO DESTROY THE LAW OR THE PROPHETS. I DID NOT COME TO DESTROY BUT TO FULFILL. FOR ASSUREDLY, I SAY TO YOU, TILL HEAVEN AND EARTH PASS AWAY, ONE JOT OR ONE TITTLE WILL BY NO MEANS PASS FROM THE LAW TILL ALL IS FULFILLED."

JESUS HEALED BECAUSE SOMEONE ASKED HIM TO HEAL

So far as the scriptures show, Jesus healed in response to requests from those who were sick, or their friends or families. The recorded instances are too numerous to recount. Four instances are: the healing of the centurion's servant (Matthew 8:5-13); of Jairus' daughter (Mark 5:22-24, 35-43); of a leper (Matthew 8:2-3); and of everyone who came to him on an occasion of his preaching. (Luke 4:40.)

JESUS HEALED BECAUSE HE ALWAYS DID WHAT HIS FATHER COMMANDED HIM TO DO

God's heart is to heal. This is evident from His self-revelation to Moses shortly after the Israelites left Egypt:

> **EXODUS 15:26**
> (GOD) SAID, "IF YOU DILIGENTLY HEED THE VOICE OF THE LORD YOUR GOD AND DO WHAT IS RIGHT IN HIS SIGHT, GIVE EAR TO HIS COMMANDMENTS AND KEEP ALL HIS STATUTES, I WILL PUT NONE OF THE DISEASES ON YOU WHICH I HAVE BROUGHT ON THE EGYPTIANS. FOR I AM THE LORD WHO HEALS YOU."

The scope of God's healing mercy is suggested in the passage from Exodus and also in Psalm 103 where David wrote:

> **PSALM 103:1-3**
> BLESS THE LORD, O MY SOUL; AND ALL THAT IS WITHIN ME, BLESS HIS HOLY NAME! BLESS THE LORD, O MY SOUL, AND FORGET NOT ALL HIS BENEFITS: WHO FORGIVES ALL YOUR INIQUITIES, WHO HEALS ALL YOUR DISEASES...

Jesus Himself healed constantly, and said of all His works:

> **JOHN 6:38**
> "FOR I HAVE COME DOWN FROM HEAVEN, NOT TO DO MY OWN WILL, BUT THE WILL OF HIM WHO SENT ME."
>
> **JOHN 12:49-50**
> "FOR I HAVE NOT SPOKEN ON MY OWN AUTHORITY; BUT THE FATHER WHO SENT ME GAVE ME A COMMAND, WHAT I SHOULD SAY AND WHAT I SHOULD SPEAK. AND I KNOW THAT HIS COMMAND IS EVERLASTING LIFE. THEREFORE, WHATEVER I SPEAK, JUST AS THE FATHER HAS TOLD ME, SO I SPEAK."

Since Jesus always did what His Father commanded and He healed all who came to Him for healing, His Father must have commanded Him to do so. It is evident also from this that God's heart is to heal!

JESUS REGARDED HIS POWER TO HEAL THE SICK AS A PROOF THAT HE WAS THE MESSIAH

Not only does the scripture show that healing is in the Atonement, but healing was also used by the Lord Jesus to prove that he was the Messiah.

At the outset of His ministry, Jesus announced in the synagogue in Nazareth that He came as a fulfillment of the prophecy in Isaiah 61 about the coming Messiah. The prophecy included healing the broken-hearted, giving sight to the blind, setting at liberty those who are oppressed. The expected Messiah was to have a healing ministry. See Jesus' comments in Luke 4:18. After reading this Scripture aloud, Jesus said, *"Today this Scripture is fulfilled in your hearing"* (Luke 4:21).

John the Baptist, although earlier convinced that Jesus was the Lamb of God who takes away the sins of the world, later from prison sent two of his disciples to ask Him: *"Are you the One who is to come, or do we look for another?"* The questioners arrived as Jesus was preaching to a crowd and healing those who were sick. Luke wrote of this encounter:

> ## LUKE 7:18-23
> AND THAT VERY HOUR HE CURED MANY PEOPLE OF THEIR INFIRMITIES, AFFLICTIONS, AND EVIL SPIRITS; AND TO MANY WHO WERE BLIND HE GAVE SIGHT. THEN JESUS ANSWERED AND SAID TO THEM, "GO AND TELL JOHN THE THINGS YOU HAVE SEEN AND HEARD: THAT THE BLIND SEE, THE LAME WALK, THE LEPERS ARE CLEANSED, THE DEAF HEAR, THE DEAD ARE RAISED, THE POOR HAVE THE GOSPEL PREACHED TO THEM. AND BLESSED IS HE WHO IS NOT OFFENDED BECAUSE OF ME."

JESUS HEALED A SICK MAN AS A PROOF OF HIS AUTHORITY TO FORGIVE SINS

This familiar event is recorded in Luke 5:20-26: Jesus was teaching in a crowded room, and men brought a paralytic on a stretcher to the house, believing that Jesus would heal him. Unable to enter because of the crowd, the men removed some tiles from the roof and let the paralytic down on ropes before Jesus. Luke writes:

> ## LUKE 5:20-26
> "WHEN HE SAW THEIR FAITH, HE SAID TO HIM, "MAN YOUR SINS ARE FORGIVEN YOU." AND THE SCRIBES AND THE PHARISEES BEGAN TO REASON, SAYING, "WHO IS THIS WHO SPEAKS BLASPHEMIES? WHO CAN FORGIVE SINS BUT GOD ALONE?" BUT WHEN JESUS PERCEIVED THEIR THOUGHTS, HE ANSWERED AND SAID TO THEM, "WHY ARE YOU REASONING IN YOUR HEARTS? WHICH IS EASIER, TO SAY, 'YOUR SINS ARE FORGIVEN YOU' OR TO SAY, 'RISE UP AND WALK?' BUT THAT YOU MAY KNOW THAT THE SON OF MAN HAS POWER ON EARTH TO FORGIVE SINS" -HE SAID TO THE MAN WHO WAS PARALYZED, "I SAY TO YOU, ARISE, TAKE UP YOUR BED, AND GO TO YOUR HOUSE." IMMEDIATELY HE ROSE UP BEFORE THEM, TOOK UP WHAT HE HAD BEEN LYING ON, AND DEPARTED TO HIS OWN HOUSE, GLORIFYING GOD. AND THEY WERE ALL AMAZED, AND THEY GLORIFIED GOD AND WERE FILLED WITH FEAR, SAYING, "WE HAVE SEEN STRANGE THINGS TODAY!"

JESUS HEALED THE SICK AS PROOF THAT THE KINGDOM OF HEAVEN WAS AT HAND, ON EARTH AND AMONG MEN

Jesus believed that two kingdoms were at war with each other on earth, the kingdom of God and the kingdom of Satan. He referred to Satan as the "enemy".

In the parable of the wheat and the tares, He said of the one who planted tares in the field: *"An enemy has done this"* (Matthew 13:28).

He regarded illness as a work of Satan. When criticized for healing a crippled woman on the Sabbath, He said:

> **LUKE 13:16**
> "...(O)UGHT NOT THIS WOMAN... WHOM SATAN HAS BOUND - THINK OF IT - FOR EIGHTEEN YEARS, BE LOOSED FROM THIS BOND ON THE SABBATH?"

Peter expressed this view, which he surely learned from Jesus, in his talk to the people gathered in the home of Cornelius. Peter commented that God sent His word:

> **ACTS 10:36-38**
> "...TO THE CHILDREN OF ISRAEL, PREACHING PEACE THROUGH JESUS CHRIST - HE IS LORD OF ALL - THAT WORD YOU KNOW, WHICH WAS PROCLAIMED THROUGHOUT ALL JUDEA, AND BEGAN FROM GALILEE AFTER THE BAPTISM WHICH JOHN PREACHED: HOW GOD ANOINTED JESUS OF NAZARETH WITH THE HOLY SPIRIT AND WITH POWER, WHO WENT ABOUT DOING GOOD AND HEALING ALL WHO WERE OPPRESSED BY THE DEVIL, FOR GOD WAS WITH HIM."

John wrote of Jesus' mission on earth:

> **1 JOHN 3:8B**
> FOR THIS PURPOSE THE SON OF GOD WAS MANIFESTED, THAT HE MIGHT DESTROY THE WORKS OF THE DEVIL.

Jesus saw this conflict as an active one. He saw Himself as carrying the message that God's kingdom is here and now. He preached, saying *"Repent, for the kingdom of heaven is at hand."* (Matthew 4:17 NKJV Emphasis added). Then He demonstrated that the kingdom was at hand by healing the sick and casting out demons.

In the same vein, Jesus told the Pharisees who suggested that He cast out demons by the power of Beelzebub:

> **LUKE 11:20**
> "BUT IF I CAST OUT DEMONS BY THE FINGER OF GOD, SURELY THE KINGDOM OF GOD HAS COME UPON YOU."

WHY SHOULD BELIEVERS PRAY FOR THE SICK?

JESUS IS OUR MODEL

> **JOHN 14:12**
> (JESUS SAID,) "MOST ASSUREDLY, I SAY TO YOU, HE WHO BELIEVES IN ME, THE WORKS THAT I DO HE WILL DO ALSO..."

The works of Jesus obviously include praying for and healing the sick.

GOD USES MEN TO RELEASE THE BLESSINGS OF THE ATONEMENT

God uses men to preach salvation.

God uses men to teach sanctification.

God uses men to exercise spiritual gifts for edifying the body of Christ.

God generally uses men to bring deliverance from demonic oppression.

God generally uses men to break the curses of poverty and hopelessness.

God can do all these things by His own supernatural power and on some occasions He does so. But for the most part He uses human beings to carry out His assignments to bring salvation, spiritual growth, deliverance, aid to the poor and hope to the hopeless.

GOD USES MEN TO RELEASE THE BLESSING OF HEALINGS

In the Old Testament, most of the recorded healings came about through the physical activity of a prophet or leader.

Some examples among many are:

Moses prayed for Miriam's healing from leprosy (Numbers 12:13).

Elisha prayed for raising the widow's son (2 Kings 4:18-37).

Elisha sent Naaman to bathe in the Jordan River for his healing (2 Kings 5:1-19).

Isaiah ordered a poultice, or medicated dressings, for Hezekiah's healing (2 Kings 20:1-11).

In the New Testament there are numerous accounts of healings worked by the Lord and through the agency of men.

The gospels are full of instances of healing by the Lord usually with the touch of His hand or other physical action.

As noted above, the Lord also sent His disciples out to preach and heal (Matthew 10; Mark 6; Luke 9; Luke 10).

Healings by believers after the Lord's ascension include:

Philip healed many in Samaria (Acts 8:5-7).

Ananias healed Paul's eyes (Acts 9:10-18).

Peter healed the lame man at the temple (Acts 3:1-8) and Aeneas at Lydda (Acts 9:32-35).

Peter raised Dorcas from the dead at Joppa (Acts 9:36-42).

Paul raised Eutycus from the dead (Acts 20:12).

Many special miracles were done by Paul in Ephesus (Acts 19:11-12).

There are few, if any, instances recorded in the New Testament of God healing through His own sovereign power without using a human agent.

Paul writes that the spiritual giftings of the Holy Spirit, specifically including gifts of healings (v. 9), are given to men for the edification of the church (1 Corinthians. 12:1-11). Certainly these gifts have been given to men because God expects men to use them!

Accordingly, if the blessings of healings that have been provided for in the atoning sufferings of Jesus are to be released among God's people and among unbelievers, those who believe in Jesus must become involved in ministering to the sick!

MINISTRY TO THE SICK IS A DEMONSTRATION OF GOD'S LOVE – OF GOD'S HEART TO HEAL

God showed His heart to heal through the life of the Lord Jesus Christ. His heart to heal is revealed in Isaiah. 61:1-4, which is referred to by the Lord in Luke 4:18-21 in the following language:

> **LUKE 4:18-21**
> THE SPIRIT OF THE LORD IS UPON ME, BECAUSE HE HAS ANOINTED ME TO PREACH THE GOSPEL TO THE POOR; HE HAS SENT ME TO HEAL THE BROKENHEARTED, TO PREACH DELIVERANCE TO THE CAPTIVES AND RECOVERY OF SIGHT TO THE BLIND, TO SET AT LIBERTY THOSE WHO ARE OPPRESSED, TO PREACH THE ACCEPTABLE YEAR OF THE LORD. ...TODAY THIS SCRIPTURE IS FULFILLED IN YOUR HEARING.

Jesus indicated repeatedly that He only said what the Father gave Him to say and He only did what He saw the Father doing. Jesus healed everyone who came to him for healing. There were no exceptions! There is no record of anyone asking Jesus for healing who was denied even when large crowds pressed upon Him.

> **MATTHEW 8:16**
> WHEN EVENING HAD COME, THEY BROUGHT TO HIM MANY WHO WERE DEMON-POS-SESSED. AND HE CAST OUT THE SPIRITS WITH A WORD, AND HEALED ALL WHO WERE SICK.

The same occasion is described by Luke as follows:

> **LUKE 4:40**
> NOW WHEN THE SUN WAS SETTING, ALL THOSE WHO HAD ANYONE SICK WITH VARI-OUS DISEASES BROUGHT THEM TO HIM; AND HE LAID HIS HANDS ON EVERY ONE OF THEM AND HEALED THEM.

God's heart clearly was to heal everyone who came to Jesus for healing.

The Psalms are full of comments by their writers that they called upon the Lord and He answered them. He delivered them out of various difficulties. In Psalm 103, David comments that God "heals all your diseases." David must have seen healings of all kinds through the intervention of God.

HEALING THE SICK IS A DEMONSTRATION OF GOD'S POWER

Jesus held authority given to Him by the Father over sickness and disease and demon oppression. In fact, He held and now holds authority over the entire world. The scripture says this in various ways. Two examples are:

> **COLOSSIANS 1:15-18**
> HE IS THE IMAGE OF THE INVISIBLE GOD, THE FIRSTBORN OVER ALL CREATION, FOR BY HIM ALL THINGS WERE CREATED THAT ARE IN HEAVEN AND THAT ARE ON EARTH, VISIBLE AND INVISIBLE, WHETHER THRONES OR DOMINIONS OR PRINCIPALITIES OR POWERS. ALL THINGS WERE CREATED THROUGH HIM AND FOR HIM. AND HE IS BEFORE ALL THINGS, AND IN HIM ALL THINGS CONSIST.
>
> **MATTHEW 28:18**
> "ALL AUTHORITY HAS BEEN GIVEN TO ME IN HEAVEN AND ON EARTH."

Jesus also was able to impart this power over sicknesses and demonic oppression to His disciples. Luke, in chapter 9 verses 1-6 says:

> **LUKE 9:1-6**
> THEN HE CALLED HIS TWELVE DISCIPLES TOGETHER AND GAVE THEM POWER AND AUTHORITY OVER ALL DEMONS, AND TO CURE DISEASES. ...SO THEY DEPARTED AND WENT THROUGH THE TOWNS, PREACHING THE GOSPEL AND HEALING EVERYWHERE.

Speaking of the occasion when Jesus commissioned His disciples to go into the towns and preach, Matthew said:

> **MATTHEW 10:1**
> AND WHEN HE HAD CALLED HIS TWELVE DISCIPLES TO HIM, HE GAVE THEM POWER OVER UNCLEAN SPIRITS, TO CAST THEM OUT, AND TO HEAL ALL KINDS OF SICKNESS AND ALL KINDS OF DISEASE.

Peter ministered healing at Lydda to Aeneas, who had been bedridden 8 years and was paralyzed, saying:

> **ACTS 9:34**
> "AENEAS, JESUS THE CHRIST HEALS YOU. ARISE AND MAKE YOUR BED." THEN HE AROSE IMMEDIATELY.

After Peter and John healed a lame man at the temple, the high priest asked Peter: "By what power or by what name have you done this?" (Acts. 4:7). Peter filled with the Holy Spirit responded:

> **ACTS 4:9-10**
> "IF WE THIS DAY ARE JUDGED FOR A GOOD DEED DONE TO THE HELPLESS MAN, BY WHAT MEANS HE HAS BEEN MADE WELL, LET IT BE KNOWN TO YOU ALL, AND TO ALL THE PEOPLE OF ISRAEL, THAT BY THE NAME OF JESUS CHRIST OF NAZARETH, WHOM YOU CRUCIFIED, WHOM GOD RAISED FROM THE DEAD, BY HIM THIS MAN STANDS HERE BEFORE YOU WHOLE."

HEALING THE SICK IS AN AID TO EVANGELISM

Healings attract attention to the evangelist's preaching and draw people to come and hear him. Healing and deliverance are evidence to the unbeliever of the power and mercy of God leading to repentance. If proper credit is given to Jesus for healings, they stir up belief in Jesus as the healer. Thus, they tend to open a way to evangelism – to believe in God and in Jesus as Lord and Savior.

HEALING AND EVANGELISM IN NEW TESTAMENT TIMES

In the ministry of Jesus, many came to Him to hear His preaching and teaching because of His healing of the sick. Among many examples, John writes of the occasion just before Jesus fed the 5,000 men.

> **JOHN 6:1-2**
> AFTER THESE THINGS JESUS WENT OVER THE SEA OF GALILEE, WHICH IS THE SEA OF TIBERIAS. THEN A GREAT MULTITUDE FOLLOWED HIM, BECAUSE THEY SAW HIS SIGNS WHICH HE PERFORMED ON THOSE WHO WERE DISEASED.

Many of those who came to hear Jesus preach and teach believed in Him because of His words. This was so even among the Samaritans.

> **JOHN 4:39, 41-42**
> AND MANY OF THE SAMARITANS OF THAT CITY BELIEVED IN HIM BECAUSE OF THE WORD OF THE WOMAN WHO TESTIFIED, "HE TOLD ME ALL THAT I EVER DID." ... AND MANY MORE BELIEVED BECAUSE OF HIS OWN WORD. THEN THEY SAID TO THE WOMAN, "NOW WE BELIEVE, NOT BECAUSE OF WHAT YOU SAID, FOR WE HAVE HEARD FOR OUR-SELVES AND KNOW THAT THIS IS INDEED THE CHRIST, THE SAVIOR OF THE WORLD."

In addition, Jesus himself said that His hearers should believe in Him because of the signs and wonders that accompanied His ministry.

> **JOHN 10:37-38**
> "IF I DO NOT DO THE WORKS OF MY FATHER, DO NOT BELIEVE ME: BUT IF I DO, THOUGH YOU DO NOT BELIEVE ME, BELIEVE THE WORKS, THAT YOU MAY KNOW AND BELIEVE THAT THE FATHER IS IN ME, AND I IN HIM."

The effect of healings on evangelistic ministry is also found in Acts, after Jesus' ascension. In Acts 3, we read of the lame man healed by Peter at the gate of the temple called Beautiful. Verse 11 reads:

> **ACTS 3:11**
> NOW AS THE LAME MAN WHO WAS HEALED HELD ON TO PETER AND JOHN, ALL THE PEOPLE RAN TOGETHER TO THEM IN THE PORCH WHICH IS CALLED SOLOMON'S, GREATLY AMAZED.

And Peter then preached to the people repentance and turning from sin.

In Acts 9, we read of Peter's healing Aeneas at Lydda, who had been bedridden eight years and was paralyzed. Verse 35 reads:

> **ACTS 9:35**
> SO ALL WHO DWELT AT LYDDA AND SHARON SAW HIM AND TURNED TO THE LORD.

At Joppa, Peter raised Dorcas from the dead. Acts 9:42 reads:

> **ACTS 9:42**
> AND IT BECAME KNOWN THROUGHOUT ALL JOPPA, AND MANY BELIEVED ON THE LORD.

Thus, these healings at Lydda and Joppa resulted in many salvations.

Paul makes a general statement about signs and wonders in his first letter to the Corinthians. After preaching unsuccessfully to the intellectuals in Athens, Paul went to Corinth where he successfully planted a vital church. He later wrote to this church:

> **1 CORINTHIANS 2:1-5**
> AND I, BRETHREN, WHEN I CAME TO YOU, DID NOT COME WITH EXCELLENCE OF SPEECH OR OF WISDOM DECLARING TO YOU THE TESTIMONY OF GOD. FOR I DETERMINED NOT TO KNOW ANYTHING AMONG YOU EXCEPT JESUS CHRIST AND HIM CRUCIFIED. I WAS WITH YOU IN WEAKNESS, IN FEAR, AND IN MUCH TREMBLING. AND MY SPEECH AND MY PREACHING WERE NOT WITH PERSUASIVE WORDS OF HUMAN WISDOM, BUT IN DEMONSTRATION OF THE SPIRIT AND OF POWER, THAT YOUR FAITH SHOULD NOT BE IN THE WISDOM OF MEN BUT IN THE POWER OF GOD.

HEALING AND EVANGELISM TODAY

C. Peter Wagner, a former professor of church growth at Fuller Theological Seminary, comments on the connection between church growth and healing by divine power in his book How to Have a Healing Ministry in Any Church.[3] Wagner comments that on average, by far the greatest church growth in the U.S. is in the churches where healing is a regular part of the

---

[3] *Regal Books, a division of Gospel Light; Ventura, California, 1988.*

ministry. He comments further that the greatest church growth in the world is in countries where healing is a regular part of the churches' ministry. He says the amazing, long current revivals in China and Argentina are sustained in large measure by churches where healing is a regular part of their ministry.[4]

In 2001, amidst the open heaven of evangelism where 500,000 lives were saved in just a few short years, visitors to the province in China were told the reason for such phenomenal church growth was the result of the people either receiving a healing or seeing someone who had been healed.[5]

One must conclude that not only did Jesus see healing as a central part of His ministry on earth, but it is also a central part of what He is doing through the Holy Spirit today.

PRAYING FOR THE SICK IS A COMMISSION FROM THE LORD

Jesus commanded His disciples to do the same thing He did – to preach that the kingdom of heaven was at hand and to prove the truth of their preaching by healing the sick.

This commission is described by Matthew as follows:

> **MATTHEW 10:1, 5, 7-8 NKJV**
> AND WHEN HE HAD CALLED HIS TWELVE DISCIPLES TO HIM, HE GAVE THEM POWER OVER UNCLEAN SPIRITS, TO CAST THEM OUT, AND TO HEAL ALL KINDS OF SICKNESS AND ALL KINDS OF DISEASE ... THESE TWELVE JESUS SENT OUT AND COMMANDED THEM, SAYING: ... " AS YOU GO, PREACH, SAYING, 'THE KINGDOM OF HEAVEN IS AT HAND!' HEAL THE SICK, CLEANSE THE LEPERS, RAISE THE DEAD, CAST OUT DEMONS. FREELY YOU HAVE RECEIVED, FREELY GIVE."

Luke says:

> **LUKE 9:1, 2, 6**
> THEN HE CALLED HIS TWELVE DISCIPLES TOGETHER AND GAVE THEM POWER AND AUTHORITY OVER ALL DEMONS, AND TO CURE DISEASES. HE SENT THEM TO PREACH THE KINGDOM OF GOD AND TO HEAL THE SICK ... SO THEY DEPARTED AND WENT THROUGH THE TOWNS, PREACHING THE GOSPEL AND HEALING EVERYWHERE.

Similarly He sent out the seventy to preach the same message in the towns where He himself intended to go. He said to them:

> **LUKE 10:8-9**
> "WHATEVER CITY YOU ENTER, AND THEY RECEIVE YOU, EAT SUCH THINGS AS ARE SET BEFORE YOU. AND HEAL THE SICK WHO ARE THERE, AND SAY TO THEM 'THE KINGDOM OF GOD HAS COME NEAR TO YOU.'"

[4] Wagner, op. cit. See chapter 3 entitled "Power Evangelism Today," starting at page 65: section "Where God is Moving," p. 70; description of evangelism in China, p. 78; description of evangelism in Argentina, p. 81.
[5] Report of Rex Burgher to Global Awakening mailing list, January 15, 2001.

These commissions were to the disciples who walked with Jesus. But it is clear that those who follow Jesus today are under the same commissioning.

At the Last Supper, Jesus said a number of things to His disciples that have generally been thought to apply to His disciples today as well. Among other things, He said to them:

> **JOHN 14:11-14**
> "BELIEVE ME THAT I AM IN THE FATHER AND THE FATHER IN ME, OR ELSE BELIEVE ME FOR THE SAKE OF THE WORKS THEMSELVES. MOST ASSUREDLY, I SAY TO YOU, HE WHO BELIEVES IN ME, THE WORKS THAT I DO HE WILL DO ALSO; AND GREATER WORKS THAN THESE HE WILL DO, BECAUSE I GO TO MY FATHER. AND WHATEVER YOU ASK IN MY NAME, THAT I WILL DO, THAT THE FATHER MAY BE GLORIFIED IN THE SON. IF YOU ASK ANYTHING IN MY NAME, I WILL DO IT."

The great commission set out in Matthew 28:19-20, originally placed on the eleven disciples, is accepted everywhere as a commission to all believers. In this commission Jesus said:

> **MATTHEW 28:19-20**
> "GO THEREFORE AND MAKE DISCIPLES OF ALL THE NATIONS, BAPTIZING THEM IN THE NAME OF THE FATHER AND OF THE SON AND OF THE HOLY SPIRIT, TEACHING THEM TO OBSERVE ALL THINGS THAT I HAVE COMMANDED YOU."

Since Jesus had sent the disciples out to heal the sick, to cast out demons, and to preach repentance saying, "The kingdom of God is at hand," His words in Matthew 28 would seem to be a commission to all believers.

This commission for all believers is also made clear in Mark 16, where Jesus said:

> **MARK 16:15, 17-18**
> "GO INTO ALL THE WORLD AND PREACH THE GOSPEL TO EVERY CREATURE … AND THESE SIGNS WILL FOLLOW THOSE WHO BELIEVE: IN MY NAME THEY WILL CAST OUT DEMONS; THEY WILL SPEAK WITH NEW TONGUES; THEY WILL TAKE UP SERPENTS; AND IF THEY DRINK ANYTHING DEADLY, IT WILL BY NO MEANS HURT THEM; THEY WILL LAY HANDS ON THE SICK, AND THEY WILL RECOVER."

Note that the signs are to follow "those who believe." This would include not only those who believed in the days of the first apostles, but all believers. If the commission to preach the gospel is still in effect for believers (which is accepted everywhere), the sign that they will lay hands on the sick and the sick will recover is also still in effect for believers.

SOME CAUTIONS

Several cautions are indicated in the New Testament that relate to the exercise of gifts of healings.

MINISTERING WITHOUT THE LEADING OF THE HOLY SPIRIT

In Matthew 7:21-23 these words of the Lord are recorded:

> **MATTHEW 7:21-23**
> "NOT EVERYONE WHO SAYS TO ME, 'LORD, LORD,' SHALL ENTER THE KINGDOM OF HEAVEN, BUT HE WHO DOES THE WILL OF MY FATHER IN HEAVEN. MANY WILL SAY TO ME IN THAT DAY, 'LORD, LORD, HAVE WE NOT PROPHESIED IN YOUR NAME, CAST OUT DEMONS IN YOUR NAME, AND DONE MANY WONDERS IN YOUR NAME?' AND THEN I WILL DECLARE TO THEM, 'I NEVER KNEW YOU; DEPART FROM ME, YOU WHO PRACTICE LAWLESSNESS!'"

The Lord seems to say that the exercise of great spiritual power, even in His own name, is not necessarily in accordance with the will of God. It is regarded by the Lord as lawlessness. Listening to the Holy Spirit and obedience to His leading are essential to this ministry.

TAKING CREDIT FOR HEALINGS

Peter (sometimes called "the teflon disciple") must be our example. After he and John healed the lame man in the temple, many excited people who witnessed or heard about the miracle crowded around them.

> **ACTS 3:1-16**
> "MEN OF ISRAEL, WHY DO YOU MARVEL AT THIS? OR WHY LOOK SO INTENTLY AT US, AS THOUGH BY OUR OWN POWER OR GODLINESS WE HAD MADE THIS MAN WALK? ... (JESUS') NAME, THROUGH FAITH IN HIS NAME, HAS MADE THIS MAN STRONG, WHOM YOU SEE AND KNOW."

Peter later repeated this statement to the high priest, rulers, elders and scribes who asked him by what authority or by what name he and John had healed the lame man.

> **ACTS 4:9-10**
> "IF WE THIS DAY ARE JUDGED FOR A GOOD DEED DONE TO THE HELPLESS MAN, BY WHAT MEANS HE HAS BEEN MADE WELL, LET IT BE KNOWN TO YOU ALL, AND TO ALL THE PEOPLE OF ISRAEL, THAT BY THE NAME OF JESUS CHRIST OF NAZARETH, WHOM YOU CRUCIFIED, WHOM GOD RAISED FROM THE DEAD, BY HIM THIS MAN STANDS HERE BEFORE YOU WHOLE."

WE SHOULD NOT BE DISCOURAGED BECAUSE NOT ALL ARE HEALED

Paul wrote to Timothy:

> **2 TIMOTHY 4:20**
> TROPHIMUS I HAVE LEFT IN MILETUS SICK.

Surely Paul and others had prayed for Trophimus but, he was not healed. Most likely not everyone you pray for will be healed. We should not take credit for the Lord's healing. Although we may pray for greater anointing for healing, we should not take on guilt when He chooses not to heal through our prayers at any particular time.

MINISTERING WITHOUT LOVE

Most important of all, in 1 Corinthians 13 Paul makes it clear that neither the exercise of the spiritual gifts, nor having all faith so as to remove mountains, nor sacrificial living profits anything unless one has love. (Verses 1-3.)

These passages seem to make it clear that the most important element in any ministry, including a ministry of healing, is love. Healing may seem to be a compassionate activity in its essence, but it can be practiced with various motivations. The believer who engages in any ministry should pray for the gift of receiving the love of God and to become a channel of God's love to those to whom he ministers.

Chapter 6
A FIVE STEP PRAYER MODEL

THE COMMISSION
HEALING WAS CENTRAL TO THE MINISTRY OF JESUS

Healing the sick was an integral part of the ministry of Jesus. In most places where the gospel speaks generally about His ministry, healing is mentioned. Matthew 4:23 is one example:

> **MATTHEW 4:23**
> NOW JESUS WENT ABOUT ALL GALILEE, TEACHING IN THEIR SYNAGOGUES, PREACHING THE GOSPEL OF THE KINGDOM, AND HEALING ALL KINDS OF SICKNESS AND ALL KINDS OF DISEASE AMONG THE PEOPLE.

Healing was also part of Jesus' assignment to the twelve disciples:

> **MATTHEW 10:1, 5, 7-8**
> AND WHEN HE HAD CALLED HIS TWELVE DISCIPLES TO HIM, HE GAVE THEM POWER OVER UNCLEAN SPIRITS, TO CAST THEM OUT, AND TO HEAL ALL KINDS OF SICKNESS AND ALL KINDS OF DISEASE ... THESE TWELVE JESUS SENT OUT AND COMMANDED THEM, SAYING, "... AS YOU GO, PREACH, SAYING, 'THE KINGDOM OF HEAVEN IS AT HAND.' HEAL THE SICK, CLEANSE THE LEPERS, RAISE THE DEAD, CAST OUT DEMONS. FREELY YOU HAVE RECEIVED, FREELY GIVE."

and to the seventy:

> **LUKE 10:1-2, 9**
> AFTER THESE THINGS THE LORD APPOINTED SEVENTY OTHERS ALSO, AND SENT THEM TWO BY TWO BEFORE HIS FACE INTO EVERY CITY AND PLACE WHERE HE HIMSELF WAS ABOUT TO GO. THEN HE SAID TO THEM, "... AND HEAL THE SICK WHO ARE THERE, AND SAY TO THEM, 'THE KINGDOM OF GOD HAS COME NEAR TO YOU.'"

> **MARK 16:15-18**
> AND HE SAID TO THEM, "GO INTO ALL THE WORLD AND PREACH THE GOSPEL TO EVERY CREATURE. HE WHO BELIEVES AND IS BAPTIZED WILL BE SAVED; BUT HE WHO DOES NOT BELIEVE WILL BE CONDEMNED. AND THESE SIGNS WILL FOLLOW THOSE WHO BELIEVE: IN MY NAME THEY WILL CAST OUT DEMONS; THEY WILL SPEAK WITH NEW TONGUES; THEY WILL TAKE UP SERPENTS; AND IF THEY DRINK ANYTHING DEADLY, IT WILL BY NO MEANS HURT THEM; THEY WILL LAY HANDS ON THE SICK, AND THEY WILL RECOVER."

Healing is part of the great commission assigned now to all believers:

Therefore, ministering in the name of Jesus to the sick, with laying on of hands, is for "those who believe." Of course this includes every member of the body of Christ!

YOUR PREPARATION

Preparation for ministry for the healing of others is very important.

Try to be a clean, clear channel for God to use!

Be "prayed up!" Pray a lot in tongues both before and during ministry time. If you don't pray in tongues, ask God fervently and specifically to be with you and to help you. He is the healer.

Take a moment to ask the Holy Spirit if there is anyone you need to forgive. If there is, forgive him or her at once from your heart. See Matthew 6:14-15.

Ask the Holy Spirit to show you any unconfessed sin in your life. If He does, repent sincerely at once and ask God's forgiveness for it. See Luke 13:2-5.

Ask God to give you His love for each person you pray for. A loving ministry will impact the sick person for good, whether or not his body is healed. He may not really know that God loves him. Your ministry may be his first experience of God's love.

Be aware that physical healing may take different routes. It may be instantaneous. It may come gradually in stages as you pray. It may come after repeated times of ministry. Or it may not come at all. God is sovereign. He heals when, how and whom He chooses in His own wisdom. Do not be put off if God does not heal someone you minister to. Our job is to pray. God is responsible for what does or does not happen.

Do not worry if the sick person does not seem to have faith for his healing. Faith helps. But God sometimes heals sick people who don't believe He can or will heal them. (And sometimes when the one who prays does not have much faith either!)

Be flexible. There is no universal rule about how to pray that will apply to all cases. There is nothing special in particular words. The Holy Spirit is the only sure guide. He may lead you differently from time to time. Practice listening to Him and following His leading.

The Holy Spirit may ask you to pray for something the person has not mentioned to you. In that case, include it in your prayer. But be clear, careful and tactful!

Review the Ministry Team Protocol and the Prayer Guidelines at the front of this Manual.

A FIVE-STEP MODEL FOR HEALING

There are different ways of praying for the sick. The following Five-Step model is not the only one. If you have found one that is effective for you, use it in your own personal ministry.

This Five-Step model is used by Randy Clark and ministry teams at Global Awakening crusades and events. It is quiet, loving and effective. It can be used by anyone.

The five steps are:

1. The Interview
2. Prayer Selection
3. Prayer Ministry
4. Stop and Re-interview
5. Post-prayer Suggestions

STEP ONE: THE INTERVIEW

Briefly interview the person requesting prayer. Be attentive and gentle. A loving attitude on your part will do much to reassure the person that he is in good hands. Ask him or her what the physical need is, but do not go into lengthy detail. For example:

"What is your name?" (A question or two to put the person at ease.)

"What would you like prayer for?"

"How long have you had this condition?"

"Do you know what the cause is?"

"Have you seen a doctor?"... "What does he say is the matter?"

"Do you remember what was happening in your life when this condition started?"

"Did anything traumatic happen to you about the time your condition began, or within a few months prior to it starting?"

[You may need to explain to the prayee why you are asking these last two questions.]

This is often sufficient for the initial interview. You may now know the nature and cause of the condition. In some cases you won't know and must ask additional questions, or simply ask the Holy Spirit for His leading. If His leading isn't clear to you, you must make an educated guess as to the nature and cause of the condition.

For example:

Perhaps there was an accident, which would usually suggest a natural cause. (But, he may need to forgive the person who caused the accident. This could mean himself, if he caused it.)

Perhaps he was born with the condition, which would often suggest a natural cause, or possibly a generational curse.

The condition may be partly or totally caused by emotional stress. Perhaps the person has had headaches ever since he lost a job. Maybe his back has hurt ever since someone cheated him. Or perhaps cancer was discovered a few months after a divorce, or after the death of a parent or child.

The cause might be spiritual. Perhaps the person has had nightmares since an occult experience he had. Maybe his condition is the result of a habitual sin, or perhaps the effect of a curse of some kind.

As noted above, if the cause is not known, ask the Holy Spirit for His leading as to the nature and possible cause of the condition. However, during your prayer for healing you may want to consider possible other causes of the condition than the one you first considered, or you may want to go back to the interview stage and ask further questions. (See the comments under Step Four on re-interviewing the person.)

STEP TWO: PRAYER SELECTION

In the prayer selection, one must decide on the appropriate type of prayer ministry.

Types of prayer ministry:

PETITION A request to heal, addressed to God, to Jesus, or to the Holy Spirit.

> "Father, in the name of Jesus I ask you to restore sight to this eye."
>
> "Father, I pray in Jesus' name, come and straighten this spine."
>
> "Father, release Your power to heal, in Jim's body, in the name of Jesus."
>
> "Come, Holy Spirit. Release your power. Touch Jim's back, in Jesus' name."

COMMAND A command addressed to a condition of the body, or to a part of the body, or to a troubling spirit such as a spirit of pain, or infirmity, or of affliction.

> "In the name of Jesus, I command this tumor to shrivel up and dissolve."
>
> "In the name of Jesus, spine, be straight! Be healed!"
>
> "In Jesus' name, I command every afflicting spirit; get out of Jim's body."
>
> "In the name of Jesus, I command all pain and swelling to leave this ankle."

A command is appropriate:

> As your initial step, unless you are led otherwise by the Holy Spirit.
>
> When there has been a word of knowledge for healing or some other indication that God wants to heal the person at this time.
>
> When petition prayers have been tried and progress has stopped.
>
> When casting out an afflicting spirit or any other spirit.
>
> When a curse or vow is broken.
>
> Whenever you are so led by the Holy Spirit.
>
> As preliminaries to praying for healing.

STEP THREE: PRAYER MINISTRY

First, audibly ask the Holy Spirit to come. You can say simply, "Come, Holy Spirit!" Or, "Come, Holy Spirit, with Your healing power." Or you may prefer a longer prayer. Then wait on Him for a minute or two.

Tell the person receiving ministry that you will be quiet for a minute or two, so that he doesn't become confused about what is going on.

AN ATTITUDE OF RECEIVING

Ask the person not to pray while you are praying for him. Here again, be gentle and loving. Say something like: "I know this means a lot to you, and you have probably prayed a lot about your condition. But for now I need you to focus on your body. I want you to just relax and to let me know if anything begins to happen in your body, like heat, tingling, electricity, a change in the amount or location of the pain, etc. If you are praying in English, or in tongues or thanking Jesus, or saying 'Yes, Yes!', it is harder for you to focus on your body. It is harder for you to receive healing."

Sometimes a person may find it very hard not to pray. Don't be hung up on this. Pray for him anyway.

If the presence of the Holy Spirit becomes evident, as by the person feeling heat or tingling or some other manifestation, continue waiting on Him until He finishes what He wishes to do at that time. When the manifestation has ebbed, check to see if healing is complete. If it is not complete, continue your ministry.

Remember: always pray or command in the name of Jesus!

You cannot use the name of Jesus too much! The power is in His name. Some who have anointed healing ministries sometimes simply repeat "In the name of Jesus," over and over as their prayer for healing.

Thank God for whatever He does. You cannot thank God too much!

MARK 16:17-18
IN MY NAME ... THEY WILL LAY HANDS ON THE SICK, AND THEY WILL RECOVER.

When you minister healing, seek to deal with the cause of the condition if you know the cause, as well as with the symptoms. For example:

> "Father, in Jesus' name I ask you to heal the cones and rods in the retina of this eye. Father, in the name of Jesus, cause the scar tissue to dissolve and leave this eye. Oh God, restore the sight in this eye, in the name of Jesus."
>
> "In the name of Jesus, I command this ruptured disc to be healed and filled with fluid, and every pinched nerve to be released and soothed. In the name of Jesus, I command the pain to leave Joe's back."
>
> "In the name of Jesus, dear God, I ask You to heal this pancreas. Father, in the name of Jesus I ask You to touch this pancreas with your healing power and cause it to function normally. Cause it to produce insulin as needed and cause all diabetes to be cured and complete health restored. Release Your healing in the name of Jesus."
>
> "In the name of Jesus, I command every afflicting spirit and every spirit of infirmity, leave Joe's body, now!"
>
> "In Jesus' name I command all stiffness to leave this joint, all pain to leave and all swelling to subside. I command all calcium deposits and all scar tissue to dissolve in Jesus' name."
>
> "In Jesus' name, I command all chemical imbalances in Joe's body to be healed.
>
> I command every organ furnishing chemicals or other signals to his organs to function normally in Jesus' name."

FORGIVENESS OF ANOTHER'S WRONG CONDUCT

If it appears that someone else caused the condition or that someone wronged the person about the time the condition started, find out if the sick person has forgiven the other. If not, forgiveness should precede your prayer for healing. Unforgiveness can be a major obstacle to healing.

If you think forgiveness is called for, ask the sick person to forgive the other, even if the sick person is not aware of any resentment toward that person.

Examples:

> A woman has had arthritis in her spine for five years, ever since her husband ran off with another woman. Has she forgiven her husband and the woman? Jesus said we <u>must</u> forgive, not we <u>ought to</u>. Emotional stress can cause illness, pre-vent healing. Sometimes one can be angry at God and must forgive Him.
>
> A pastor has had back pain for ten years. Ten years ago there was a split in his church and some of his closest friends turned against him. Has he forgiven the ringleaders of the split, his former friends, and all others involved?
>
> (Note: Sometimes a person is healed before you even begin to pray for healing, just by forgiving the person who caused the hurt, or just by repenting and asking God's forgiveness for his own sin of resentment and anger. The pastor noted above was healed by forgiving without any prayer for healing.)

REPENTANCE FOR ONE'S OWN WRONG CONDUCT AND ASKING FORGIVENESS FOR IT

If it appears that the condition was brought on by sin, very gently inquire if the person agrees that this might be so. If he does, encourage him to repent and ask God's forgiveness. This should precede your prayer for healing. Sin that is not repented for can impede healing. Anger can contribute to back pain and some depressions. AIDS may result from a wrong lifestyle. Lung cancer might have been caused by smoking.

But, be tender. Ask if perhaps the condition could be related to his lifestyle. Perhaps say, "I wonder if this condition could be related to things you have done in the past." Never accuse the person confrontationally of causing his condition by his sin. It is seldom helpful and you may be wrong.

> *A caution: If this leading is of the Holy Spirit, the Holy Spirit will usually indicate the specific sin which is the problem, not sin in general. General accusations of sin are often destructive and probably are from the enemy.*

A person may need to forgive himself. He may have caused his own injury or sickness. This may seem unnecessary but it sometimes releases healing.

SOME PRACTICAL SUGGESTIONS ON HOW TO MINISTER

If changes in the seeker's condition can be readily determined, it is appropriate and often helpful to pray short prayers or give brief commands interspersed with re-interviewing at frequent intervals to see if progress is being made.

> "What has happened to the pain now?"
>
> "See if you can read the sign now."
>
> "Do you still feel heat in your stomach?"
>
> "Try moving your knee now."

(A person may be partly or completely healed without feeling anything. He may not realize that healing has taken place until he uses the affected part. If he does something he could not do before or that caused pain before, he can see if the prayer thus far has made a difference.)

When a prayer or command results in a partial healing, continue to use it until you find that it no longer produces further healing.

Two examples of short prayers with frequent interviews, in actual situations, are set out in Examples 1 and 2 at the end of this section.

Note that many of the prayers or commands for healing set out in scripture are very short.

> "I am willing. Be cleansed." (Mark 1:41)
>
> "Little girl, I say to you 'Arise.'" (Mark 5:41)
>
> "God, be merciful to me, a sinner!" (Luke 18:13)
>
> "Please heal her, O God, I pray!" (Num. 12:13)

> "In the name of Jesus Christ of Nazareth, rise up and walk!" (Acts 3:6)
>
> "Jesus the Christ heals you. Arise and make your bed." (Acts 9:34)
>
> "Brother Saul, the Lord Jesus, who appeared to you on the road as you came, has sent me that you may receive your sight and be filled with the Holy Spirit." (Acts 9:17)

If a long prayer is followed by partial healing, it is hard to know what part of the prayer or command was effective. Then if it is to be repeated, the entire prayer may have to be repeated.

However, short prayers are not always called for. Where progress cannot readily be determined, such as with diabetes, frequent interviewing is not useful unless there are manifestations which help you to know what is going on. For example, if there is heat and the heat intensifies with certain prayers, then short prayers with frequent interviews may be appropriate.

Even if short prayers are appropriate, healing may not come after the short prayers. But healing will sometimes come after an extended time of prayer or after many prayers or after several times of praying.

BE PERSISTENT

If you try one kind of prayer or command and get results but not complete healing, continue. Explain why you are continuing to the person receiving prayer or he may wonder about the repetition. Be persistent!

If you try one kind of prayer or command and get no result after a few times, try another kind! Be persistent!

Sometimes a person expects you to pray only once for his condition and then stop. So if he is not healed promptly, he may expect you to stop praying and he may start to leave. Encourage him to stay and let you pray more. Continue praying as long as God seems to be making any further change in his condition or as long as you are given different ways to pray for him. Be persistent!

If healing has partially come and then seems to stop, wait a bit. Continue praying for a time to see whether another wave of healing will come. Be persistent!

YOUR MANNER

You need not necessarily pray aloud all the time. If you wish, tell the person that you may pray silently at times. As long as you have your hand on his arm you are praying, even if not aloud.   And do pray silently. Listen to the Holy Spirit. He may give you some guidance you would otherwise miss.

It is often very helpful to pray with your eyes open, and observe the person you are praying for. Look for signs that God is at work in his body: fluttering eyelids, trembling, perspiration. If you see something happening or if the person reports a change in the pain or increased sight or other progress, thank God for what He is doing and bless it. Continue to pray in the manner that led to the progress.

If you are not accustomed to praying with your eyes open, this will require practice! However, it is worth the practice as it sometimes helps you see what God is doing.

Use your normal tone of voice. Shouting or praying loudly in tongues will not increase your effectiveness.

Don't preach, don't give advice and don't prophesy.

STEP FOUR: STOP AND RE-INTERVIEW

If after a time you are making no progress, consider interviewing the person further.

Possible questions might be:

"Would you try again to remember whether anything significant happened within six months or so of the beginning of this condition?" (Some event may require forgiveness that the person may have forgotten or may have been unwilling to disclose.)

"Do any other members of your family have this condition?" (If so, perhaps there is a generational spirit affecting several members of the family.)

"Do you have a strong fear of anything?" (Fear can be a cause of many physical and spiritual problems, and it sometimes interferes with healing.)

"Is anyone in your family a member of the Freemasons or Eastern Star?" (Association with Masonic or other occult organizations is particularly likely to impede healing.)

"Has anyone ever cursed you or your family that you know of?"

"Have you had other accidents?" (If the person is accident-prone, consider whether he is under a curse.)

"Have you ever participated in any kind of occult game or practice?"

See Chapter 9 (Page 81) of this manual entitled Hindrances to Healing.

CONSIDER WHETHER A WRONG SPIRIT MAY BE PRESENT

If the person reports that the pain has moved or has increased, it signals the likely presence of an afflicting spirit. Simply command the afflicting spirit to leave in the name of Jesus. You might pray with more intensity, but not louder. "In the name of Jesus, I break the power of this afflicting spirit and command it to leave Joe's body!" Or an equivalent prayer.

If the condition has existed a long time or if it is a condition that resists medical treatment such as cancer, diabetes, Parkinson's, AIDS, etc. Consider that there is likely to be a spirit causing the condition or resisting healing and command it to leave. "In the name of Jesus, I command any spirit of arthritis to leave this woman!"

(When expelling a spirit of infirmity or an afflicting spirit or a spirit of a particular condition, a simple prayer may be enough. But see section on "Deliverance" for help in cases where expelling a spirit seems more difficult.)

INNER HEALING

Very often a person who requests prayer for a physical problem is also in need of emotional healing from hurts and wounds suffered as a result of trauma, physical or emotional abuse, perceived or real rejection, disappointments, fears, perceived or real inadequacies, and so on. These hurts and wounds may have accumulated over a long period of years.

Sometimes the physical healing of such a person cannot be fully realized unless and until his inner wounds and hurts have been healed or a process of healing begun.

Sometimes, even if a person seems to receive physical healing it may be apparent that emotional healing is also needed.

Sometimes the person thinks his problem is physical, or sometimes you or he may think he needs deliverance. However, what he really needs is inner healing.

In these cases, you should by all means take time to pray for the person's inner healing. Follow the leading of the Holy Spirit. Pray for the healing of hurts that have become apparent in your conversation with the sick person. If you are so led, inquire gently about the causes of the inner hurts. If circumstances permit, take time to understand the situations at least in general. If time is limited, consider scheduling another session with the sick person.

Pray for the healing of each specific hurt just as you would for each specific physical ailment.[1] It is appropriate to inquire from time to time whether the Holy Spirit has put additional specific needs on the person's mind that you might pray for.

Allow the prayee to weep. Encourage it if he begins to cry. Let God love, comfort and console the person through you. When emotions are very strong, it is often helpful to ask Jesus to speak to the person or to show him how Jesus sees his situation. You may know other effective methods of praying for inner healing.

MINISTRY TO A PERSON WHO IS UNDER MEDICAL CARE

You will have occasion to minister to people who are consulting with a counselor or psychiatrist. This probably is not a problem if your ministry is for a physical ailment such as a broken limb or back pain. However, if healing for emotional problems is indicated, you should ask the

[1] Francis McNutt says specificity is particularly important in prayer for inner healing.

prayee to get the approval of his doctor or counselor for his seeking prayer. This is especially important if the prayee is under medication.

Sometimes a person under medication, such as for diabetes, asthma, arthritis, heart disease, etc., believes he has been healed when you pray for him. He may think he can discontinue his medication. You must instruct him to continue his medication after your ministry to him; even if he believes and even if you believe he has been healed. He must return to his doctor and let the doctor change his medication if the doctor considers it appropriate to do so.

MINISTRY TO A PERSON WITH MULTIPLE PROBLEMS

As a general rule, it is better to finish praying for one condition before starting to pray for another unless the Holy Spirit directs you differently. Flitting from one problem to another is distracting. The person's faith will be built up for successive problems if one healing is completed.

The sick person may ask you to pray for a second problem as soon as you finish your first prayer for one condition. He may not understand that you will pray further for the first condition. Tell him gently that you will pray for the second condition. But first you wish to finish praying for the first condition.

Follow the leading of the Holy Spirit! If you are praying for a person's sinus infection and his bad foot begins to tingle, stop praying for the sinus condition and pray for the foot. Bless what God is doing and pray in cooperation with what He is doing. Go back to the sinus only when you have finished praying for the foot or when the sinus begins to manifest the presence of God at work there.

OTHER

Ask the Holy Spirit for His leading and expect to receive it.

Don't cause guilt in the person you are ministering to. Don't make him feel guilty if he does not get healed. Don't tell him it is his fault even if you think it is!

If you think you may have made a mistake don't fret over it. The Holy Spirit is bigger than your mistakes!

If possible, always use a catcher. A person may fall even though you are praying only for his physical healing. If you don't have a catcher, have the prayee sit down or stand against a wall so that he cannot fall or have the person stand in front of a chair so that if he becomes weak he can settle into the chair.

If the prayee falls, pray for him a few moments longer and then see if he has been healed ("How is the pain now?" "Try moving your neck now." etc.). Ask if he senses that the Holy Spirit is still touching him. If he senses that God is still at work in him, pray further for him. If nothing seems to be happening, ask the Holy Spirit whether you are through praying for him and continue as long as the Holy Spirit wants you to.

WHEN TO STOP PRAYING

Stop praying when:

The person is completely healed.

The person wants you to stop. He may be tired or simply feel you should stop.

The Holy Spirit tells you it is time to stop.

You are not given any other way to pray and you are not gaining ground.

STEP FIVE: POST-PRAYER SUGGESTIONS

After praying, consider the following:

Encourage the prayee's walk with the Lord.

You might share a scripture verse. For some people, scriptural passages are extremely meaningful and encouraging.

If a condition resulted from occult experiences or habitual sin, suggest tactfully that a change in lifestyle may well be needed to avoid a recurrence of his condition.

If he is not healed or not completely healed, don't accuse him of lack of faith for healing or of sin in his life as the cause.

Encourage the person to get prayer from others if there is little or no evidence of healing, or if his healing has not been completed. Encourage him to come back again for more prayer after the next meeting, etc. Sometimes healing is progressive and sometimes it occurs only after a number of prayers for healing have been made.

Tell the prayee not to be surprised if he experiences a spiritual attack after a healing. Help him to be prepared to resist it. If a symptom starts to recur, he can command it to leave in Jesus' name. If a bad habit is involved, he may be tempted for a short time to re-commence the habit. If he does yield, quick repentance is needed and asking God's help to overcome.

LOVE! LOVE! LOVE!

As a minister of healing, do everything in love.

AN OBSERVATION

If you pray for more people, you will see more people healed!

EXAMPLE 1: SHORT PRAYERS ON BACK PAIN

BACK PAIN

Example of an interview and prayer exchange between a pray-er (**P**) and a person with severe back pain (**A**). This illustrates the use of short prayers interspersed with interviews. It is a closely approximate account of an actual event.

THE SITUATION

A comes to **P** with a friend for help with a bad back. **A**'s back hurts so much that she has to ease herself down into a chair when she sits down and has to struggle painfully to stand up again.

THE PRELIMINARY STEPS

P: "Where does your back hurt?"

A: (Pointing.) "All across this part of my back."

P: "When did your back start hurting?"

A: "About three months ago."

P: "Do you know what caused it?"

A: "I hurt my back moving some furniture."

P: "Have you seen a doctor about this?"

A: "A chiropractor. He treats me for a vertebra that has slipped out of place."

P: "Has he helped you?"

A: "Yes, each time I see him. But the pain comes back and it's getting worse."

P: "Did you need help moving the furniture?"

A: (Bitterly) "I asked my husband to help me move it but he wouldn't. He never helps me with anything around the house."

P: "Do you need to forgive him?"

A: "I suppose so."

P leads **A** in a prayer of forgiveness for her husband for not helping to move the furniture, releasing him to God, undertaking not to try to change him herself, and blessing him.

NOTE: At this point **P** could have led **A** in a prayer forgiving her husband for <u>all</u> the hurts he has

59

caused her. This should be done at some point. If it not done now, **P** should suggest that **A** do this soon.

> **P**: "Now let's take a reading on your back. Try moving it. How is the pain now?" **A** moves her back.
>
> **A**: (Surprised.) "Well, it's a lot better!"
>
> **P**: "Is the pain completely gone?"

Note: anger is a frequent cause of or contributor to back pain. Sometimes a person is completely healed just in the act of forgiving the one who has caused the pain.

> **A**: "No, but it's a lot less."
>
> **P**: "Well, now let's pray for it. Let me check your legs first."

THE MINISTRY

P checks **A**'s legs and finds that one is a little shorter than the other. **P** prays for the short leg to lengthen, which it does. **P** asks **A** to stand up and see if the pain has changed in her back.

> **A**: "Well, it's still better. But I get a twinge right here." (A touches her back.)
>
> **P**: Puts his hand on the spot that hurts. "*In the name of Jesus, I command all pain to leave A's back*. Now try your back again."
>
> **A**: "It's good. Very good."
>
> **P**: "Is the pain all gone?"
>
> **A**: "I would say just about all. It's some stiff and sore."
>
> **P**: (Puts his hand on **A**'s back.) "*In the name of Jesus, I command every spirit of pain or soreness or stiffness to get out of A's back.* Now let's check it again."

In this case, the pain was now completely gone and the prayer ended. **P** asks **A** to thank Jesus for healing her.

NOTES

If the pain had not completely gone, **P** might have given one or more of the following commands until the pain left completely, or until there was no more progress.

"that all the vertebrae in **A**'s back line up properly, one squarely on top of the other."

"that all the discs in **A**'s back take their proper size and shape and location."

"that every pinched nerve be released, and every damaged nerve be healed."

"that all extra calcium deposits or growths in **A**'s back dissolve and be gone."

Also, if **A** had a pain running down one of her legs, it is likely to be from a pinched or damaged sciatic nerve. If such a pain develops at the time that **P** is praying for **A**'s back, it may be caused by a spirit of sciatica. **P** could pray as follows, as appropriate:

"In the name of Jesus, I command **A**'s sciatic nerve to be healed."

or,

"In the name of Jesus, I command the spirit of sciatica to get out of **A**'s body."

(After praying in this way, **P** would check for change in the pain.)

In the real case, **P** then asked **A** to pray a prayer of thanksgiving and asking the Holy Spirit to come and fill **A** up.

In this case, **A** was encouraged to walk continually in forgiveness of her husband. Her back was still well after about 8 months. So it appears that the healing was permanent.

This example is not intended as a comment on other types of prayer for healing. God uses all types of prayers. As one example, God sometimes heals with the simple prayer, "God, please heal Sally." Or, "Sally's back be healed, in the name of Jesus!" See Moses' prayer for Miriam: *"Please heal her, O God, I pray!"* (Numbers 12:13.)

Similarly, it is not intended as a comment on longer prayer times. There are some situations that call for unhurried longer prayer times. Also, even if short prayers are appropriate in a given situation, if healing does not come soon longer prayer times may result in healing.

The point of the above example is simply that praying short prayers with frequent interviews is often an effective way to pray and can result in healing within a rather short time frame.

EXAMPLE 2: SHORT PRAYERS ON PERSON WITH INJURY TO CHEST AND ARM MUSCLES, AND INABILITY TO LIFT ARM

[An example of exchanges between a person with pain, weakness in some of his left arm and chest muscles, inability to raise his left arm to shoulder height (**A**) and the person praying for him (**P**). This also was an actual situation with a successful conclusion.]

THE INTERVIEW

P: (After **A** has explained his condition.) "How did this all happen? Did you have an accident?"

A: "I'm a courier. I was delivering a package for a messenger service and ran into a thick glass door that I thought was open. I hit my shoulder and bent my arm. I was really stupid. It was my fault. I was partly drunk. Now I can't lift a heavy package or ride a bicycle. I can't lift my arm above this high (demonstrating). So, I can't get any kind of a job that requires much use of my arm."

P: "When did this happen?"

A: "About seven years ago."

P: "Have you forgiven yourself for being drunk and for running into the door?"

A: "No, it hasn't occurred to me that I need to forgive myself."

THE MINISTRY

P: "Well, let's do it anyway."

P leads **A** in a prayer of repentance for taking alcohol into his body and asking God's forgiveness, and of repentance for being partly drunk, for being careless as a courier, asking God's forgiveness and forgiving himself for the whole incident.

> **P**: "Now check your chest muscles and see how they are. See how high you can raise your arm."
>
> **A**: "The pain in my arm is nearly gone! My chest still hurts. I think I can lift my arm higher." **A** tries lifting his arm. He can lift it a bit higher, but not much.
>
> **P**: "All right. That's good! Now let's pray for your healing. First, we'll ask the Holy Spirit to come. We'll all just be quiet for a minute or two. You don't have to pray. Just relax and let the Holy Spirit do whatever He would like to do at this time. *Holy Spirit, please come with Your healing power.*"

Everyone is quiet for a minute or so. **A** feels heat in his chest. **P** thanks God for what He is doing. When the heat subsides, **A** still has pain in his chest, slight pain in his arm and cannot raise his arm higher than the last time he tried.

> **P**: "Let's pray for the pain in your chest muscles." **P** lays his hand lightly on **A**'s chest. "*In the name of Jesus, I command **A**'s chest muscles to be healed. I command all bruising to leave and the effect of all the past bruising to be healed.* Now check your chest and see if the pain has changed either for the worse or the better."
>
> **A**: "The pain in my chest is much less. It's almost gone now too."
>
> **P**: (Repeating) "Well, that prayer seemed to make some progress, we'll pray that one again. *In the name of Jesus, I command **A**'s chest muscles to be healed. I command all bruising to leave and the effect of all the past bruising to be healed, in Jesus' name!* Now check again to see if anything further has happened to the pain."
>
> **A**: "The pain in my chest is completely gone!"
>
> **P**: "Try pushing on my hand and see if your arm or chest hurts."

A pushes on **P**'s hand and says the arm and the chest do not hurt. **P** says to push harder. **A** pushes very hard on **P**'s hand but has no pain.

> **P**: "Well, thank Jesus for healing your arm and chest! You know He is the healer."
>
> **A**: "Yes, I will!"
>
> **P**: "Let's do it right now."
>
> **A**: "Thank you Jesus for healing my arm and chest."
>
> **P**: "I think you will find the strength has returned to your arm. However, if it isn't com-pletely healed, come back and get prayer for it again another time."
>
> **A**: "Thanks, I will!"
>
> **P**: "Now let's pray for your arm movement." **P** lays his hand on **A**'s shoulder. "*In the name of Jesus, I command **A**'s arm to be healed. In Jesus' name, I command all the muscles and ligaments in his arm to function normally so that he can raise his arm normally.* Now try raising your arm."

A tries to raise his arm with somewhat more success but not a lot more. **P** repeats his prayer until improvement stops.

P: "I'm going to raise your arm with my hand but I don't want to hurt you. You tell me at once if this hurts."

P raises **A**'s arm a bit. "Does that hurt?" **A** says it doesn't hurt, so **P** raises the arm farther.

"Does this hurt?" **P** repeats this once more and **A** says the arm hurts a little. **P** holds the arm up and commands the pain to leave.

> **P:** "Okay. Now you see if you can raise your arm that much."
>
> **A:** "Well, I can't raise it as far as you did, but much more than I could before."
>
> **P:** repeats lifting **A**'s arm until there is slight pain and commanding the pain to leave. **A** gains a little more lift when trying to raise his arm.
>
> **P:** "Just in case there is one present I'm going to cast out any spirit of infirmity in your arm. *In the name of Jesus, I command any spirit of infirmity in* **A** *or in his arm to get out of him now! In the name of Jesus, I command any afflicting spirit to get out of him now! Your assignments are over*! Now, try your arm again."
>
> **A:** "This is amazing! I can't raise it all the way, but almost. And it doesn't hurt at all."

P prayed three or four more times for healing of the muscles and ligaments in **A**'s shoulder. He lifted **A**'s arm until **A** felt discomfort and then commanded the muscles and nerves to be healed and the pain to leave. Eventually, **A** had complete move-ment of his left arm without pain. It seemed that he was completely healed. **P** had **A** thank Jesus for healing him and then prayed for filling with the Holy Spirit and a general prayer of blessing over **A**.

NOTES

After eight or nine months, **A**'s arm still had full movement and its strength had returned. It seems that his healing was permanent.

Chapter 7
WORDS OF KNOWLEDGE FOR HEALING

WHAT IS A WORD OF KNOWLEDGE?

A word of knowledge is a supernatural revelation of information by the Holy Spirit. Paul received many of his revelations through words of knowledge.

> **1 CORINTHIANS 2:12-13**
> NOW WE HAVE RECEIVED, NOT THE SPIRIT OF THE WORLD, BUT THE SPIRIT WHO IS FROM GOD, THAT WE MIGHT KNOW THE THINGS THAT HAVE BEEN FREELY GIVEN TO US BY GOD. THESE THINGS WE ALSO SPEAK, NOT IN WORDS WHICH MAN'S WISDOM TEACHES BUT WHICH THE HOLY SPIRIT TEACHES ...

WORDS OF KNOWLEDGE FOR HEALING

The Holy Spirit often gives a revelatory word of knowledge concerning the need of a person (or more than one person) for healing. This is an indication that God wishes to heal the person or those who have the condition revealed in the word of knowledge, and usually at the time the word is given. When understood in this way, a word of knowledge builds faith in the person who needs the healing and also in the person who received the word of knowledge. Accordingly, the person who received the word should normally speak it out at the time or at the next appropriate time seeing if it applies to someone present. If so, offer to pray at once for that person's (or their) healing.

SPECIFICITY IN WORDS OF KNOWLEDGE FOR HEALING

The more specific the word of knowledge is, the more faith it builds in the people involved. If the word is received through feeling a pain, it is helpful if the kind of pain and its exact location is stated. For example:

> It is better to say, "A shooting pain on the left side of the neck just below the ear," or to point to the exact location, than to say merely, "A pain in the neck," or, "Does someone's neck hurt?"
>
> It is better to say "Pain in the third lumbar vertebra" or to point to the exact location than to say merely, "Back pain."
>
> It is better to say, "Ringing in the left ear," if that is the word, than to say, "Trouble with an ear."

The person receiving the word should be careful not to change it and not to add to it. He should not exaggerate nor should he leave out a detail that seems unimportant to him. Changes or additions cause confusion. For example:

A person had a mental picture of someone being injured by tripping over a green hose. The only green hoses he had seen were garden hoses. So he said he had a picture of a person injured by tripping over a green garden hose.

There was a man in the meeting who had been injured by tripping over a green pressure hose at work. He did not respond to the word at first, because the hose he tripped on wasn't a garden hose. He would have responded more quickly if the person receiving the revelation had not added to it.

THE TIMING OF WORDS OF KNOWLEDGE

You may receive a word of knowledge anywhere and at any time. You might get a word during a prayer meeting, a cell group meeting, walking past someone in church, in the supermarket or while washing dishes at home.

You may or may not know for whom the revelation has been given.

Most often, the word of knowledge is given for someone present. However, it may be for someone not present but whom someone present knows about. Or it can be for someone you will see in the next day or so.

HOW TO SPEAK WHEN YOU BELIEVE YOU HAVE RECEIVED A WORD OF KNOWLEDGE FOR HEALING

At first, it is generally wise to be tentative in speaking out the word you have received. In a small meeting you might say, "Does anyone have a sharp pain in his left elbow just now?" If no one responds, don't be concerned. If someone responds you could say, "Well, I just had a sharp pain in my left elbow, which may be a word of knowledge indicating that God would like to heal you now since you have that condition. Would you like for me (or us) to pray for you now?"

If the person is open to receiving prayer, pray for him. If he wants prayer later, pray for him later. If he doesn't want prayer due to embarrassment, lovingly encourage him to receive. But if he refuses, don't pressure him in any way to receive prayer.

If you believe you have received a word of knowledge for healing in a large meeting, you probably would not speak out unless there is an appropriate moment indicated by the leader. But you would "keep your antennae up" to see whether God puts someone across your path later on who has the condition revealed to you. If He does, you can have confidence that God wants to do some healing work in the person you discover.

HOW DOES GOD GIVE WORDS OF KNOWLEDGE FOR HEALING?

God gives His revelations in different ways and that is true of words of knowledge for healing as well as for other kinds of revelation. Some of the more common ways He gives words of knowledge for healing are:

FEELING

You may have:

> a sharp pain in some part of your body,
>
> a throbbing sensation,
>
> some other sensation,
>
> a strong emotion such as fear or panic.

Be careful that your feeling is not caused by a condition in your own body. For instance, if you often have pain in your left ear, you would not give that as a word of knowledge even if you get that pain during a meeting.

SEEING

You may get a mental picture, such as:

> a body part -- perhaps a heart, a foot, an eye, a head,
>
> a person with a certain condition such as a limp,
>
> a person carefully holding his arm,
>
> a crutch, eye-glasses, a person walking with a cane,
>
> a water bottle, a barbed wire fence, an auto accident.

READING

You may see in your mind:

> a person with a word written across his front or back, or over his head,
>
> a word written on a wall or on a carpet,
>
> something like a newspaper headline or a banner.

AN IMPRESSION ("THINKING" THE WORD.)

You may sense in your mind that someone has a particular condition or that the Holy Spirit has spoken the word to you. It is a mental impression.

SPEAKING

While talking or praying or standing with someone, unpremeditated words may tumble out of your mouth relating to a physical condition you were not aware of.

A DREAM

You may have a vivid dream or vision in which:

> you have a new health problem,
>
> you see someone with a health problem,
>
> you hear someone talking about a health problem.

EXPERIENCE IT

Similar to dreaming it, you may have a vivid vision while awake. It may be so strong that you are actually a part of what is happening, not just an observer.

Sometimes these categories blend together. Is it a mental picture or a vision? Vision could be likened to a "3D Technology movie or virtual reality" - something given by the Holy Spirit that is beyond a mental picture in intesity and vividness.

SOME PRACTICAL INSIGHTS TO HELP YOU GROW IN THE USE OF WORDS OF KNOWLEDGE FOR HEALING

A word of knowledge for healing may come quickly, flitting through your mind more like a bird or dancing butterfly than like a stationary billboard.

It may be rather vague, tempting you to screen it out, to ignore it. Practice "tuning in" to these revelations and speaking them out. If you are tentative and humble, not arrogant or presumptuous, no one will be offended if you seem to have heard amiss.

Resist the thought that a word you have received is not important or that it is "just you." Remember, it builds faith in the other person to know that God has revealed his condition to you. What seems like a vague impression to you may be a shout to the other person!

However, don't be presumptuous. Don't say, "God just told me you have an earache."

Instead, say,

> "Does your left ear ever bother you?"
>
> "I have an impression of a problem in a left ear. Does this mean anything to you?"

Other examples:

> "Does a picture of a flower vase mean anything to you?"
>
> "I think I see a picture of cows in a field. Does that have any significance for you?"

Be as specific as the word revealed to you. The more specific the word, the more it builds faith in you and in the other person or people.

Unpretentious honesty is the best policy! It's perfectly okay:

> to admit that you're nervous,
>
> to say that you have only a vague impression,
>
> to say that you have never had a word for someone before,
>
> to say that praying for sick people is new to you.

Don't be afraid. Don't let fear rob you and the person who might have been healed. Someone has said that "faith" is spelled "r-i-s-k," Be patient, but step out! Be humble, but step out! Be tentative, but STEP OUT! God is giving you words of knowledge because He wants you to use them! He wants you to use them wisely, prudently and humbly. But He does want you to use them.

WORDS OF KNOWLEDGE FOR HEALING AS AN AID TO EVANGELISM

Many people are accustomed to the idea of prayer for healing in the sense that folks in church or in a prayer group will pray for the healing of someone who is sick in the hospital or at home. There is often no expectation of prayer in the presence of the sick person or of immediate healing for the sick person. Usually the most that is expected is that the sick person's recovery may be shortened a bit. Even if recovery is shortened somewhat, this type of experience is not especially impressive to unbelievers.

However, healing on the spot, in the name of Jesus, can have considerably more impact. It can result in people responding to Jesus who otherwise might never do so. It is a demonstration of the power of God in the name of Jesus. It is a demonstration that Jesus is concerned about people and about their illnesses. It can be an avenue of hope for a person who has given up hope. It can be proof that the name of Jesus is more powerful than the workings of Satan.

Words of knowledge for healing can be an especially effective aid to evangelism. They clearly seem to be intended by the Lord for immediate healing. For the person who is not born again to experience immediate healing as a result of a word God gave someone for him or who sees someone else healed in that way, the experience can be a striking evidence of the power and love of God.

If you are present at such a time, don't overlook the possibility that someone present may be encouraged by the healing to make a first commitment to Jesus or a deeper commitment to Him.

Chapter 8
HEALING OF SOME SPECIFIC CONDITIONS

OBSTACLES TO HEALING

This section assumes that obstacles to healing which are connected to the beginning of the illness will be dealt with in the preliminary steps of the ministry.

Typically these will be forgiveness of others, repentance, asking forgiveness for one's self and the like.

PHYSICAL CONDITIONS IN WHICH IMPROVEMENT CAN BE DETERMINED READILY

With some conditions, improvement or change can readily be assessed. These include many conditions of pain such as pain in the ankle, leg, or arm; pain in the back or neck; pain in a joint, as from arthritis; etc. They also include stiff or immovable joints, inability to perform some common motions such as bending over and straightening up again, blindness and deafness.

In the case of such conditions, very short prayers are appropriate, each followed by a question to see whether the prayer brought movement of the pain, lessening or worsening of the pain or other condition prayed for, or other change. As noted in the general section on healing, if a prayer seems to be effective bless what God is doing and repeat the prayer until progress stops. The person ministering might begin with such prayers or he might begin with a general prayer for healing and move on to more specific prayers if the general prayer does not result in complete healing.

The method followed in these examples can be used in any situation where improvement or change in the sick person's condition is readily apparent to the observer or to the person receiving ministry. Several such situations are listed on the following pages with some steps the person ministering might follow if he uses this method.

Preliminaries to the Specific Ministry

In most of the following cases, the person ministering should interview the person seeking healing (who is generally called "**A**" in the following paragraphs) and should ask the Holy Spirit to be present. This might be in the following way:

The Interview

> Ask when the condition started.
>
> Find out the cause if **A** knows what the cause is.
>
> Ask if **A** has seen a doctor. If so, what the doctor says the cause is.
>
> Ask if any significant event or events occurred about the time the pain started.
>
> If so, have **A** deal with any issues of forgiveness or repentance involved.

Ask the Holy Spirit to be Present

Then say something like: "Now we'd like to ask the Holy Spirit to come with His healing power. Then we will be quiet for a minute or two to see if the Holy Spirit touches you in some way. You don't need to pray, just relax and receive.

Holy Spirit, please come and touch **A** with your healing power."

Let the Holy Spirit do what He Wishes to Do

Now you can be quiet for a minute or two, then ask A if he feels anything in any part of his body. **A** may feel heat or tingling, or he may tremble or perspire. This may be in the part of his body for which he requested prayer or it may be somewhere else. If there is any manifestation of the working of the Holy Spirit, you should simply continue remaining quiet and let the Holy Spirit complete whatever He wants to do. You will want to speak to the prayee occasionally just to assure him that ministry is continuing. You will want to thank the Holy Spirit aloud for what He is doing.

A may be completely healed when the above steps (called "the preliminaries" in the following sections) are completed. If he is not completely healed, ministry can continue along the lines set out below for specific kinds of disease.

In the suggestions made in the following sections, each suggested prayer and each suggested command should be made "in the name of Jesus". Remember that the healing power is in His name. There is no virtue in other specific words. The substance of the suggested prayers is the important part. Use these notes as a starting point and add to them as you are given additional insights or leading.

BACK PAIN

See Example 1 in the preceding section for a detailed actual example of ministry for back pain.

If the pray-er (**P**) has checked the length of **A**'s legs, **A** is probably sitting. **P** might ask that the prayee (**A**) remain sitting. **P** can put his hands on **A**'s feet or hold them while praying. Or he might ask the prayee to stand, check for any change in the back pain, and pray while placing his hand on the prayee's back.

NECK PAIN

The steps are the same as for back pain.

P might stand in front of **A** with his hands on the sides of **A**'s face and **P**'s fingers on or alongside the spinal column in **A**'s neck. Or **P** may simply stand at **A**'s side with his hand on **A**'s neck.

PAIN OF UNKNOWN CAUSE IN ANY PART OF THE BODY

After the preliminaries,

Command:

Healing of the specific cause of the condition.

> That the pain leave.
>
> That any spirit of pain leave.
>
> That any afflicting spirit leave.
>
> That any torn or bruised bone, muscle, ligament or other tissue be healed.
>
> That any damaged nerve be healed.
>
> That any abnormal calcium or cartilage or other abnormal tissue dissolve.
>
> That any other damaged tissue be healed.
>
> Such damaged tissue could be a bone, muscle, nerve, tendon, blood vessel, cartilage, etc.

PAIN KNOWN TO BE CAUSED BY A BRUISE, FRACTURE, STRAIN, ETC.

Same as above, for pain.

Other prayer steps:

> That the bruise be healed.
>
> That the swelling go down.
>
> That the injured blood vessels be healed.
>
> That the fracture be healed.
>
> That the various types of damage caused by the strain be healed.

HEADACHE (OTHER THAN A MIGRAINE HEADACHE)

After the preliminaries,

> Command the headache to leave.
>
> Command any spirit of headache to leave.
>
> Command the blood vessels in the back of the neck to relax, open up, and release the pressure in **A**'s head.
>
> Ask the Father to heal any injury and to release any fear that may be causing **A**'s headache.

SHORT ARM OR SHORT LEG

A difference in the length of one's legs is often related to back problems.

A difference in the length of one's arms can be related to back problems and may be related to respiratory problems.

A difference in the length of arms can be determined by asking **A** to stand erect with his feet pointing straight forward, hold his arms out straight with his elbows locked, arms out as far as they will go, and his hands about a quarter to a half inch apart. Then have him bring his hands together so they won't move with respect to each other and bend his elbows. Now he can see from the tips of his fingers whether one arm is longer than the other.

The difference in the length of legs can be determined by asking **A** to sit in a straight-back chair with his hips as far back as they will go and his legs straight. Then you can gently lift his legs off the floor and check the heels of his shoes. The heels of his shoes will reveal any difference in the length of his legs.

You must be careful in lifting **A**'s feet off the floor. Sometimes if there is a back problem, lifting **A**'s feet very much can cause excruciating pain. Don't lift his feet high enough to cause pain.

An alternate way of checking the comparative length of legs is to place a thumb squarely on each ankle bone, holding the arms and thumbs in a straight line and then check whether your thumbs are even.

If legs appear to be of different lengths, this may actually be the case or the apparent difference can be caused by a tipping of the pelvis. In either case, you can pray the same way. The correction can come by lengthening of the short leg or by movement of the pelvis into its proper position.

The ministry:

> Command the short arm or short leg to grow out.

If the short arm or leg does not respond quickly, have **A** move the arm or the leg and then check it again.

Note: the preliminary steps ordinarily would be skipped in short arm or short leg cases. However, if the shortness was caused by an accident, there may be a party to the accident that **A** needs to forgive.

DEAFNESS

After the preliminaries,

> Command healing of the specific cause of the condition.
>
> Cast out the spirit of deafness.
>
> Cast out any deaf and dumb spirit.

Command:

> Healing of the auditory nerve.
>
> Replacement of lost nerve hairs in the inner ear.
>
> Release of bones in middle ear that have grown together.
>
> Healing of any damaged bone in middle ear.

EYES - BLINDNESS

After the preliminaries,

> Command healing of the specific cause of the blindness.
>
> Command eyes to open up and see.
>
> Cast out any spirit of blindness.

Command:

> Healing of the retina, cones, rods and nerves.
>
> Healing of the optic nerve.
>
> Healing and restoration of the anatomy due to the degeneration to the macula area.
>
> Removal or absorption of any edema or blood

EYES - CATARACTS

(Condition caused by drying out of the fluid between layers of the lens so that the layers cannot slide over each other.)

After the preliminaries,

> Command healing of the specific cause of the condition.
>
> Command the lens to clear, for all the opacities, cloudiness, for nothing to block the rays of light from passing through the lens.
>
> Cast out any spirit of blindness or cataracts.

EYES - GLAUCOMA

(Condition caused by too much pressure inside the eyeball which destroys the nerve cells.)

After the preliminaries,

Command:

> The pressure in the eye to return to normal.
>
> Normal functioning of the organs controlling pressure in the eye.
>
> Healing or restoration of the nerve cells damaged by high pressure.
>
> Cast out any spirit of glaucoma.
>
> Cast out any spirit of blindness.
>
> Cast out any spirit of infirmity and any afflicting spirit.

EYES - CROSSED

After the preliminaries,

> Command healing of the specific cause of the condition.
>
> Command eyes to straighten out.
>
> Command weak eye muscles to strengthen or the muscles to be in balance.
>
> Cast out any spirit of blindness; of crossed-eyes; of infirmity.
>
> Command the eyes to focus properly.

EYES - ASTIGMATISM, SHORT-SIGHTEDNESS, FAR-SIGHTEDNESS

After the preliminaries,

> Command healing of the specific cause of the condition.
>
> Cast out spirit of astigmatism (or of near-sightedness or of far-sightedness).
>
> Astigmatism - Command the cornea to be healed, to have equal curvature all around the cornea.
>
> Near-sightedness – command the axial length of the eyeball to shorten.
>
> Far-sightedness – command the axial length of the eyeball to lengthen.
>
> Command flexibility to the lens as when they were a child.

ARTHRITIS

<u>Note</u>: anger, unforgiveness and especially bitterness seem to play a large part in many cases of arthritis. It can be anger, unforgiveness and bitterness toward himself as well as toward others.

If the prayee does not recall any event calling for forgiveness or any person he needs to forgive (including himself), have him pray a general prayer of forgiveness of others and of himself. Then have him renounce the spirits of anger, resentment and bitterness. Break their power over him and cast them out.

Command healing of any specific known cause of the arthritis.

Cast out:

> Any spirit of arthritis.
>
> Any spirit of inflammation.
>
> The spirit of pain.

Command:

> All pain to leave.
>
> All inflammation to be healed.
>
> All swelling to be gone.

ASTHMA

After the preliminaries,

Command:

> Healing of any specific known causes of the asthma.
>
> Any spirit of asthma to leave.
>
> Any spirit of fear or anxiety and any generational spirit to leave.
>
> Any spirit of allergies to leave.
>
> Opening of bronchial tubes, lungs, air sacs.
>
> Strong functioning of immune system.

CARPAL TUNNEL SYNDROME

After the preliminaries,

Command:

> Healing of any known cause of the condition.
>
> The wrist tunnels to open up and release pressure on nerves and tendons.
>
> Swelling of the tunnel tissue to subside.
>
> Any inflammation of the tendons, nerves, tunnel to subside.
>
> Swelling of the tendons to subside.
>
> Any spirit of inflammation to leave.
>
> Any spirit of pain to leave.
>
> The pain to go.
>
> All scar tissue to be dissolved.

BOWED LEGS

After the preliminaries,

Check the length of the legs. Pray for any short leg to lengthen.

> Command the legs to straighten.
>
> Command the muscles on the outside of the legs to function normally.
>
> Command the tendons on the outside of the legs to tighten.

FEVER

After the preliminaries,

Command:

> The healing of any known cause of the fever.
>
> The fever to leave.
>
> Any spirit of fever to leave.
>
> The temperature control mechanisms of the body to function normally.
>
> All infection to be healed.
>
> The immune system to function strongly against all infection.

SCIATICA

After the preliminaries,

> Pray as for back pain.
>
> Command healing of any known cause of the sciatica.
>
> Cast out the spirit of sciatica.

CRACKED TAILBONE

The cause usually is a fall. If another person caused the fall, he may need to be forgiven. If **A** caused the fall, he may need to forgive himself.

After the preliminaries,

Command:

> Healing of any known cause of the fracture, if it wasn't caused by a fall.
>
> The pain to go.
>
> Any spirit of pain to go.
>
> The fractured parts to come together in proper alignment; knitting of the bones.
>
> Healing of any damaged tissue.

VARICOSE VEINS

After the preliminaries,

> Command healing of any known cause of the condition.
>
> Cast out any spirit of inheritance, of varicose veins, of infirmity.
>
> Command any blockage of the flow of blood in the veins to be removed.
>
> Command the walls of the veins to strengthen and function normally.
>
> Command the blood to flow normally back to the heart.

In cases where short prayers of the kind suggested above do not result in healing, one may repeat the process, change to "soaking" prayer, pray in tongues, or pray generally for healing, perhaps at considerable length.

WHEN HEALING DOES NOT SEEM TO BE HAPPENING READILY

There is a large class of diseases in which the prayee will not know, from change in symptoms at the time he receives prayer, whether or not he has been healed or helped.   In these diseases, pain may not be present when prayer takes place. If pain is not present, **A** usually cannot recognize any change in his condition. For this reason, the method of praying short prayers with frequent interviewing is usually not useful.

This is not to say that there cannot be an indication that healing is taking place.

Sometimes the prayer for healing may result in manifestations the prayee or even the pray-er can recognize such as trembling, fluttering eyelids, heat, sweating, tingling, or electricity.

The pray-er (**P**) can ask the prayee (**A**) at intervals whether manifestations are happening in **A**'s body. If manifestations are taking place, they encourage both **P** and **A** to thank God for what He is doing and to continue the prayer.

However, the absence of manifestations does not always mean that nothing is happening. Sometimes healing takes place without any manifestation and the prayee may not realize that he has been healed for a time. For example, an X-ray may be required to show the healing, or the prayee may go several days without the inter-mittent pain that he had before receiving prayer.

Since the pray-er is proceeding without the signposts that show whether or not healing is occurring even as he is praying he may want to be quite thorough in his prayers. He may want to "cover all the bases." He may want to spend some time just "soaking" the prayee in love and prayer. He may want to spend some time praying in tongues.

Also, he may want to be sure to have some time quietly listening to the Holy Spirit for any guidance the Holy Spirit wants to give him. He should follow up on any leading of the Holy Spirit. For example, if he receives an impression that there has been some kind of event in **A**'s life, such as an accident or loss of a family member or some occult experience, he should inquire of **A** whether indeed such an event has occurred. Under such circumstances, if such an event has occurred, **P** can be sure that the Holy Spirit is telling him that the event is significant in connection with **A**'s illness.

In addition, sometimes there are conditions in the prayee's life which he may not consider relevant to his illness but which in fact may be very relevant. (And they may not have been mentioned in the initial interview.)

For example:

> Anger, resentment and unforgiveness are often associated with back pain.
>
> Unforgiveness and bitterness are sometimes associated with arthritis.
>
> Stress and tension can contribute to many illnesses.
>
> Fear can contribute to or even cause many illnesses.
>
> Unforgiveness can block healing.
>
> Occult experiences not renounced generally will block healing.
>
> A curse, suspected or unsuspected, can block healing.
>
> Inherited tendencies can cause or contribute to illness.

Some feel that anxiety, self-hatred, self-rejection, shame, guilt and low self-esteem can contribute to or cause some illnesses.

When praying for an illness or condition which does not readily permit immediate assessment of the presence or absence of healing, the pray-er may want to carefully consider the above and perhaps additional factors. He may want to use a checklist for review or he may be able to hear clearly from the Holy Spirit as to whether or not such influences are present.

Further suggestions as to a few specific diseases follow:

CANCER

After the preliminaries,

> Command healing of all known causes of the cancer.
>
> Cast out the spirit of cancer.
>
> Cast out any spirits of infirmity or affliction.
>
> Curse the cancer cells, root and seed. Command them to shrivel and die.

Command:

> The immune system to function strongly against cancer cells.
>
> Healing to any body parts damaged by the cancer.
>
> The bone marrow to produce healthy blood cells.

DIABETES

After the preliminaries,

> Ask if **A** has any feelings of rejection, self-hatred or guilt. If so, seek the root of such feelings, lead him in prayers of repentance and forgiveness of himself or others. Have him renounce the spirits involved, break their power and cast them out.
>
> Command the healing of any known cause of the diabetes.
>
> Cast out the spirits of diabetes or infirmity.
>
> If indicated, cast out the spirit of inheritance, break generational curse.
>
> Command a new pancreas into **A**'s body.
>
> Command that any body parts damaged by excess blood sugar be healed.

Chapter 9
SOME HINDRANCES TO HEALING

SUMMARY

Sometimes when healing does not occur, there are hindrances that can be discovered and dealt with so that healing can take place. Many of these potential obstacles to healing are not likely to be discovered in the short initial interview that normally takes place when someone wishes to receive prayer for healing.

If a hindrance is present but is not found in the initial interview, it may still be discoverable. A parent, sibling or friend accompanying the sick person may speak of it. The pray-er may ask further questions during the prayer session. The sick person may volunteer information. The Holy Spirit may help you. Questions prompted by the Holy Spirit can lead to removal of hindrances that otherwise might not be discovered.

Some of the more common hindrances are listed below and discussed on the following pages.

Unforgiveness.

Resentment, anger, bitterness.

Lack of needed inner healing.

A curse.

Generational problems.

Past involvement in the occult.

Lack of desire for healing.

Freemasonry.

Difficulty in believing that God heals today.

Fear.

Unresolved guilt.

Disobedience.

Unbroken inner vows.

Ungodly soul ties.

Belief that God imposed the illness to develop the sick person's character.

Sin in the sick person's life.

Presence of a spirit of illness or affliction.

A NOTE ABOUT CASTING OUT SPIRITS WHEN PRAYING FOR THE SICK

Normally, casting out a spirit related to an illness is a simple and short process of commanding the spirit to leave in the name of Jesus. Sometimes a spirit may be stubborn and refuse to leave readily or it may begin to manifest by talking to the pray-er, causing the sick person to become sleepy or in other ways discussed in the section of this manual on deliverance. For suggestions as to how to handle such more difficult situations, see the section on deliverance.

DISCUSSION

UNFORGIVENESS

Unforgiveness is a common and effective blockage to healing. In the initial interview, when the sick person is asked when his condition began and whether some significant event happened about the time it began, some event for which the sick person blames someone he has not forgiven may be disclosed.

There may be other persons – parents, relatives, friends, others -- who have offended, hurt, or injured the prayee whom the prayee has not forgiven. Their offending conduct is not always perceived by the sick person as related to his condition.

If the sick person is unwilling or unable to forgive someone, you should explain that unforgiveness can prevent his healing. (But be careful not to promise healing if he does forgive.)   It should be explained to him that forgiveness is a choice – a decision – not necessarily a feeling. He can forgive another without having a warm feeling toward the other. It should be explained to him that if he does not forgive the other person, God will not forgive him his own trespasses.

> **MATTHEW 6:14-15**
> "FOR IF YOU FORGIVE MEN THEIR TRESPASSES, YOUR HEAVENLY FATHER WILL ALSO FORGIVE YOU. BUT IF YOU DO NOT FORGIVE MEN THEIR TRESPASSES, NEITHER WILL YOUR FATHER FORGIVE YOUR TRESPASSES."
>
> **MATTHEW 18:35**
> "SO MY HEAVENLY FATHER ALSO WILL DO TO YOU, IF EACH OF YOU, FROM HIS HEART, DOES NOT FORGIVE HIS BROTHER HIS TRESPASSES."

Sometimes there is a spirit of unforgiveness that can be cast out and releasing the prayee to forgive.

Forgiveness can be important even if the sick person is not aware of any wrong attitude. For example, a person suffered whiplash because someone struck his car in the rear at a stop sign. It had not occurred to him to forgive the person driving the other car. Yet, he was healed simply by forgiving that person without further prayer.

Forgiveness should be accompanied by a choice to leave any change in the other person up to God. That is, the sick person should stop trying, even in thoughts and attitude, to change the other person (if indeed he is making such an effort). Forgiveness should also be accompanied or followed by a prayer of blessing on the other person. Real forgiveness is achieved when the injured person genuinely desires God's blessing on the other.

RESENTMENT, ANGER, BITTERNESS, RAGE

Resentment, anger, bitterness and rage often accompany unforgiveness. If so, in addition to forgiving the other person, the passions of resentment, anger, bitterness and rage may need to be renounced. In addition spirits of resentment, anger, bitterness and rage may need to be cast out.

LACK OF NEEDED INNER HEALING

Resentment, anger and bitterness often are the fruit of severe hurt, real or imagined. Giving up the resentment, anger and bitterness and forgiving the other person who caused the hurt, may not by themselves bring the needed healing of the broken heart or bruised spirit. Always consider whether the Holy Spirit would have you pray for healing of these wounds before praying for healing of the physical condition.

Grief, pain, hopelessness or despair may also impede healing and may often be resolved by loving prayer for inner healing.

A CURSE

A curse is an invocation of evil upon someone through spoken or written words such as: an intentional curse spoken in a fit of rage or in a long-running quarrel, or imposed by incantations of a witch doctor, or by demonic rituals as in voodoo.

A curse can be imposed unintentionally by words spoken over the person receiving ministry or over his family, either by himself or by a third person. For example, if the person had a sickly childhood, it is possible that a frustrated parent might have said something to him along the lines that he has a weak constitution and will always be sick. Or, if a number of members of a family have had cancer, the sick person might have said of himself or herself something like: "All the women in my family have had cancer and I'll probably get it too."

If a specific curse is identified, it should be broken. For example, "In the name of Jesus, I break the curse of every word spoken to Jim by his father, that _____ (mentioning the type of words spoken by his father). I cancel any effect those words have had or may have on Jim's health."

If a specific curse cannot be identified, but it seems that one or more may exist, all curses should be broken in a general prayer. All jewelry, paraphernalia or symbols of freemasonry which the individual has purchased or inherited should be destroyed. Also, see Chapter 10 of this manual on "Curses".

GENERATIONAL TENDENCIES

Inquiry can be made as to whether other family members have or have had the same illness and particularly whether ancestors have had it. If so, cast out all spirits related to the inherited disease and cut the person from his inherited tendency to the illness. Then pray for healing. For example: "In the name of Jesus I command every spirit of diabetes to get out of Jim. I break the power of any spirit of diabetes passed on to Jim by his ancestors. In the name of Jesus, I cut Jim from his ancestors in every way that is not of the Lord Jesus. In the name of Jesus, I command all damage to Jim's pancreas to be healed and I command his pancreas to function normally."

PAST INVOLVEMENT IN THE OCCULT

Involvement in occult practices always opens the door for demonic oppression of some form. In the opinion of some with considerable experience, prior occult involvement always hinders or prevents healing. Such involvement should be repented of, renounced and forgiveness requested. Then any spirit involved should be expelled. Then pray for healing.

LACK OF DESIRE FOR HEALING

The sick person may feel that there are some advantages to being sick that out-weigh his desire for healing. There can be financial advantages, such as disability compensation, which may seem more attractive to him than the prospect of going to work each day which he would have to do if healthy. There may be relationship advantages, such as the sympathy, comfort and coddling of relatives or friends. There may be an emotional advantage, such as an excuse for failure in a job or relationship. Such considerations, whether conscious or unconscious, may persuade the sick person that he is better off sick than well and may interfere with healing.

In some cases, even though he does not want healing, the sick person may desire and seek prayer for healing, either because he does not recognize his true feelings or perhaps to gain attention and sympathy even while not wanting effective help.

The sick person's real feelings may not come out immediately. If the Holy Spirit suggests that this is a problem, the person ministering may explore the situation gently by inquiring about the circumstances. The remedy is intercession. The pray-er may feel led to pray aloud that God will heal the prayee's emotions and restore God's perspective on his situation.

FREEMASONRY

Freemasonry is actually a religion that competes with Christianity. Its god is a combination of Jehovah, Baal and Osiris. As such, it is idolatry and an occult religion. In addition, Freemasonry requires of its adherents a number of oaths of secrecy each accompanied by terrible curses for violation of the oaths.

Participation in Freemasonry very often results in curses of various kinds, not only on the individual involved but also spreading out through his family in any direction. Illness in one person can be caused by Freemasonry in a relative for example.

If Freemasonry is present in the family of a person whose healing is difficult, the freemasonry should be renounced and all curses related to it broken. Any objects, icons or symbols of freemasonry which the person may have purchased or may have inherited should be destroyed.

DIFFICULTY IN BELIEVING THAT GOD HEALS TODAY

In some religious systems people are taught that God does not heal today – that healing was present in the early church for various reasons, but that it is not present today. Such people often have no difficulty believing that God can heal if He wishes to and they may believe that God has in fact healed some people. But they may believe that such healings are truly exceptional and they may have considerable doubt that God is willing to heal the person himself.

Many such people are sincere Christians and believers in the Bible as the Word of God. In such a case, the pray-er may seek to impart faith for healing into the sick person by referring to the basic scriptures on healing and pointing out that Jesus is the same yesterday, today and forever. He may mention that healing is in the Atonement, just as salvation is, according to the scriptures. Testimonies of healing can be helpful.

FEAR

Fear can be the cause of many problems both physical and emotional. It can cause torment, despair, hopelessness and other conditions in addition to physical problems. Frequently, there is a spirit of fear that has entered through trauma or childhood experiences. Fear can also be a strong deterrent to healing.

Where there are strong fears, usually the oppression of a spirit of fear is involved. See the chapter on Deliverance for suggestions on dealing with a spirit of fear.

UNRESOLVED GUILT

The sick person may think he is unworthy of being healed. This of course is true in the sense that healing is entirely of God's grace and not earned. But a conviction that his unworthiness will prevent healing indicates a lack of grasp of the forgiveness available in the Atonement. Explanation of the work of Jesus in the Atonement, discussion of some of the scriptures on healing and prayer for assurance of forgiveness and salvation may help the prayee overcome his feeling of unworthiness and guilt.

DISOBEDIENCE

Healing can be impeded if the sick person is stubbornly disobeying some leading that God has given him. The remedy in such a case is repentance, asking forgiveness and dealing with any spirit of disobedience if one is involved, followed by obedience if obedience is still possible.

However, healing has always been a powerful influence in evangelism due to the healing not only of believers but of unbelievers, as well. Some who pray extensively for both believers and unbelievers report that they have a higher success rate with unbelievers than they have with believers.

UNBROKEN INNER VOWS

The sick person may have made inner vows that have not been broken. For example, he may have had a sickly parent who complained much about his condition and the sick person may have vowed never to admit being sick. Or he may have found as a child that being ill was an excuse for not doing assigned tasks and may have resolved to be ill whenever life's circumstances presented him with distasteful duties.

UNGODLY SOUL TIES

The sick person may be under the influence of a close friend or relative who does not believe the sick person will ever be well. Or who does not want the sick person to be healed. Ties of this sort must be renounced and broken.

THE PRESENCE OF A SPIRIT OF INFIRMITY OR AFFLICTION

Long illness or an incurable illness often is accompanied by spirits of infirmity or affliction or disease that try to impede healing. They should be cast out.

THE BELIEF THAT GOD HAS CAUSED THE SICKNESS TO DEVELOP THE SICK PERSON'S CHARACTER

God of course can use sickness to develop character or for other purposes, but our Lord always viewed sickness as a work of the devil and never hesitated to heal. Showing the person some of these scriptures may help him overcome this problem.

SIN

Some sicknesses are the result of abuse of one's body or other sin. In such cases, prayer for healing should be preceded by confession, repentance and asking forgiveness. Examples might be lung cancer if caused by smoking, or a sexually transmitted disease if acquired through immoral conduct.

The person with lung cancer caused by smoking should confess the sin of abusing his body by smoking, repent of it, ask God's forgiveness, and renounce smoking for the future. Then the ministry of prayer for healing would follow.

If a sexually transmitted disease was acquired through immoral relationships, the person with the disease should confess those sins, repent of them, ask forgiveness and give up that lifestyle. This would be followed by prayer for his healing.

Wrong conduct contributing to an illness can be affirmatively committing a known sin, failing to obey a clear commandment or leading of the Lord or wrong attitudes or emotions.

Chapter 10
CURSES

WHAT IS A CURSE?

DEFINITION

One dictionary definition of "curse" is: a prayer or invocation for harm or injury to come upon a person; an imprecation; a malediction. It may be a pronouncement of doom or of an evil fate or vengeance. People who minister to those under a curse add that a curse has a spiritual or demonic power to work evil.

A curse is commonly thought of as something intended by one person to have a significant evil effect on another person. However, a curse can be unintentional. A curse can be self-inflicted.

The term "curse" is sometimes used to mean not specifically the imprecation itself but the harm or injury that follows an imprecation or the state of a person where a series of unfavorable or disastrous circumstances indicate that the person is "under a curse".

Also, a curse can be a general malaise in a house or other place induced by a demonic icon. Some icons are idols; demonic symbols in tapestries, china or other decorations; totem poles; hideous statuettes; distorted images; or objects that have been worshipped.

TYPES OF CURSES

GENERAL OR SPECIFIC

A curse can be general or it can be intended to result specifically in any one or more of a long list of unfortunate conditions or disasters, including, sickness, barrenness, severe social or economic misfortune, susceptibility to accidents, fears, torment and death.

CONDITIONAL OR UNCONDITIONAL

A curse can be conditional or unconditional. A conditional curse is intended to take effect only on the happening of the stated condition. An example of conditional curses are the invocation of terrible physical harm on one's self by members of a Masonic lodge or of a satanic cult for breaking its rules of secrecy. It is presumed by those who make these vows of secrecy that if they are careful to observe their vows, the curses will not fall upon them.

Many examples of conditional curses can be found in the Old Testament. One example are the curses that the Lord indicated He would impose on the Israelites for disobedience to His commands. See Deuteronomy 28:

> **DEUTERONOMY 28:15**
> BUT IT SHALL COME TO PASS, IF YOU DO NOT OBEY THE VOICE OF THE LORD YOUR GOD, TO OBSERVE CAREFULLY ALL HIS COMMANDMENTS AND HIS STATUTES WHICH I COMMAND YOU TODAY, THEN ALL THESE CURSES WILL COME UPON YOU AND OVERTAKE YOU: ...

For a New Testament example of a conditional curse, consider one of the hard sayings of the Lord:

> **MATTHEW 25:31-33, 41-43, 45-46**
> WHEN THE SON OF MAN COMES IN HIS GLORY, AND ALL THE HOLY ANGELS WITH HIM, THEN HE WILL SIT ON THE THRONE OF HIS GLORY. ALL THE NATIONS WILL BE GATHERED BEFORE HIM, AND HE WILL SEPARATE THEM ONE FROM ANOTHER, AS A SHEPHERD DIVIDES HIS SHEEP FROM THE GOATS. AND HE WILL SET THE SHEEP ON HIS RIGHT HAND, BUT THE GOATS ON THE LEFT. ...
>
> "THEN HE WILL ALSO SAY TO THOSE ON THE LEFT HAND, 'DEPART FROM ME, YOU CURSED, INTO THE EVERLASTING FIRE PREPARED FOR THE DEVIL AND HIS ANGELS: FOR I WAS HUNGRY AND YOU GAVE ME NO FOOD; I WAS THIRSTY AND YOU GAVE ME NO DRINK; I WAS A STRANGER AND YOU DID NOT TAKE ME IN, NAKED AND YOU DID NOT CLOTHE ME, SICK AND IN PRISON AND YOU DID NOT VISIT ME ...
>
> INASMUCH AS YOU DID NOT DO IT TO ONE OF THE LEAST OF THESE, YOU DID NOT DO IT TO ME.' AND THESE WILL GO AWAY INTO EVERLASTING PUNISHMENT ...

Examples of unconditional curses are those imposed by a witch or a witch doctor intended to impose illness, disaster, death or other harm upon an enemy of the witch's or witch doctor's client. These are intended to operate irrespective of the circumstances.

INTENTIONAL OR UNINTENTIONAL

The above examples are of intentional curses, where the person invoking the curse knows what he is doing and intends to place a curse upon his target. However, a curse can be unintentional. See, the notes on curses resulting merely from careless statements set out in the section below on how curses are generated.

SELF-IMPOSED OR IMPOSED BY OTHERS

Most curses are probably imposed by others, generally by enemies of the person cursed, or by an agent of the enemy, such as a witch or witch doctor. However, a curse can be self-imposed. A person can also impose a curse on himself by careless words.

GENERATIONAL CURSES

A curse can be passed on from one generation to another. Note the curse imposed "on ourselves and on our children" by the crowd at Jesus' trial. The curse of leprosy Elisha placed on Gehazi for his greed and dishonesty in dealing with him and Naaman (whom Elisha had healed of leprosy) was this:

> **2 KINGS 5:27**
> THEREFORE THE LEPROSY OF NAAMAN SHALL CLING TO YOU AND YOUR DESCENDANTS FOREVER.

Curses from occult practices tend to be generational. Some illnesses and addictions seem to run in families and may be caused by a curse. See particularly the comments about Satanic cults and Freemasonry in the following sections.

WHAT IS THE EFFECT OF A CURSE?

As noted above, a curse typically has spiritual power. It often has the effect intended by the one who invokes it and it may have other effects, as well. It can cause the conditions listed above or other evils. This spiritual power is not derived from God but from Satan. A curse is "something said or done against us or others which **gives rights to the demonic to exercise power over people.**"[1] (Emphasis added.)

However, apart from their intended effect unbroken curses can have other effects such as to impede or prevent healing or deliverance. They may also cause a general malaise resulting in poor health, lack of success in one's occupation, financial problems, family difficulties, etc.

A conditional curse can have evil effects not related to the stated condition of the curse. Membership in a secret society or in a Satanic cult can bring a curse of its own, on the person involved or on his family, even if the person involved faithfully performs all his promised duties. Usually, if the person involved is trying to get free of a curse, he has already left the society or organization and the actual conditions of at least some of the curses he has imposed on himself have been met.

Even if the member of the organization is faithful to his vows, the demonic nature of his activity can and often does give rise to a curse. It is a frequent observation that membership in

---

[1]Horrobin, _Healing Through Deliverance (Revised and Expanded)._ Chosen Books, Grand Rapids, MI, 2008, p. 426. An extended discussion of the sources and other aspects of curses: pp. 424-439.

a Masonic organization can bring evil not only upon the member himself but also on his extended family. If a family exhibits unusual multiplicity of problems, such as multiple illnesses, premature deaths, divorces, addictions and accidents, it is always appropriate and often very helpful to interview the person for the possibility of membership – his own membership or that of an ancestor or other relative – in a satanic organization or in a secret society, particularly in a Masonic organization.

Because it has demonic power, the bondage of a curse lasts indefinitely until it is broken. If a curse is present, it often must be dealt with before a successful prayer for healing or deliverance can take place. Although this is not a hard and fast rule.

HOW ARE CURSES GENERATED?

It will help in dealing with curses if we understand how they are generated. Among the common ways are these four: intentional imprecations or curses, which may be written or oral; careless statements not intended as curses but which nonetheless have spiritual power to cause harm to the person at whom they are directed; involvement with a secret society or an occult activity or organization; conduct that brings a curse upon the performer. In addition, there are other phenomena that operate somewhat like a curse such as the iniquities of ancestors that are passed on to descendants.

INTENTIONAL CURSES IMPOSED BY OTHERS

Some curses are generated intentionally by enemies of the person cursed.

A person with a grievance against another may curse the other or may engage a witch or witch doctor to place a hex or charm or imprecation on the other. In some cultures, it is common to ask a witch doctor to curse an enemy.

SOMEONE MAY CURSE ANOTHER IN THE HEAT OF RAGE OR HATE

Persons or families involved in violent quarrels, especially if protracted, may curse each other. Some cultures are known for the prevalence of the placement of intentional curses on families or clans. For example the Scottish clans, Arabic families and families in some sections of the United States have historically engaged in vicious cycles of attack and retaliation against each other frequently invoking curses upon each other.

The spread of satanic activities in North America has brought increased awareness of the practice of adherents to these organizations of imposing curses on Christians and others. Also, such organizations frequently have occult practices that can result in curses, such as vows of various kinds, contracts with Satan or with each other, marriage to Satan, etc.

Comment has been made above of the curse placed by the Lord Jesus on those who ignore the needs of the poor.

SELF-IMPOSED INTENTIONAL CURSES

An example of a self-imposed intentional curse is that of members of secret societies as referred to above. Masonic organizations are particularly well-known for vicious, sick curses of the latter type. In addition, members of secret societies may have taken vows of other kinds that can produce curses.

Some of us persist in self-condemnation for words or actions God has forgiven. These can eventually result in a demonic bondage.

CARELESS STATEMENTS NOT INTENDED AS CURSES

A curse can be unintentional. For example, a curse can result from careless words spoken by a parent, in exasperation or frustration about the inability of his child to understand something or to perform an act to the parent's satisfaction. Such careless words may actually be curses affecting the future of the child.

> You can't do anything right!
>
> You are just plain stupid.
>
> You'll never amount to anything.
>
> You'll never be able to hold a job.
>
> You'll probably be sick all your life.
>
> No one would ever marry you.

Such pronouncements can sink into a young person's mind and become a spiritual bondage – a demonic bondage – resulting in exactly the condition described by the parent. This type of curse can be placed on a person by anyone in authority over him such as a teacher, an army officer, an employer, as well as by a parent.

The power of such pronouncements is recognized in Proverbs.

> **PROVERBS 15:4**
> **A WHOLESOME TONGUE IS A TREE OF LIFE, BUT PERVERSENESS IN IT BREAKS THE SPIRIT.**
>
> **PROVERBS 18:21**
> **DEATH AND LIFE ARE IN THE POWER OF THE TONGUE...**

Unintended curses can be self-imposed by careless words as well. Some examples are:

> She drives me crazy.
>
> I get sick every time I think of that.
>
> I would like to die.
>
> I'm scared to death of becoming poor.
>
> I'm embarrassed to death.
>
> Cross my heart and hope to die...

INNER VOWS

A somewhat different kind of curse can be self-imposed by a person who is so deeply offended by someone else's conduct that he vows never to engage in such conduct. A child may be so offended by a parent's conduct – controlling the household by going into rages over small things, for example – that the child vows inwardly never to engage in the offensive conduct. Such vows can sometimes create a demonic bondage that the child cannot overcome and he finds himself engaging in the same conduct that offended him so much in his parent.

PARTICIPATION IN SECRET SOCIETIES

Mere participation in some activities can have significant adverse effects on the person himself and on his family. Mention has been made above of Satanic cults and of Freemasonry. For example, the extended families of Freemasons frequently exhibit what seems to be the effect of a curse, such as unusual numbers of divorces, incurable illnesses, addictions, accidents and premature deaths.[2] Sometimes an activity by a Freemason seems to have a corresponding effect on a family member. For example, one particular Masonic ritual involves placing a noose around the member's neck. A member of the family of such a member had difficulty in breathing until an apparent curse related to that noose was broken.

One ministry with extensive experience in healing has found that Freemasonry in a family is frequently present when a member of the family has one of several specific diseases or conditions which resist prayer for healing or deliverance[3].

CONDUCT THAT BRINGS A CURSE

Conduct that brings a curse often has a spiritual dimension such as participating in occult practices of a satanic cult or disobedience to a command of God. There are a number of passages in the Bible that deal with curses placed upon a person or group because of the conduct of the person or group.

Note that Deuteronomy 27 and 28 detail a number of types of conduct that can result in curses, either for an individual or for a group.

INIQUITIES OF ANCESTORS

Where an ancestor has habitually or flagrantly sinned in a particular way, efforts to heal a person sometimes have the same difficulty as if a curse were involved. These may be cases described by God when He declared His nature to Moses on the occasion of the giving of the second set of the Ten Commandments on Mount Sinai.

---

[2]For a number of specific examples, see Cassada, _Unto Death. Freemasonry – Freedom in Christ or Bondage to Lucifer?_, Maryville, TN 1998.
[3]Cassada, op. cit., p. 37. Listed are approximately two dozen such diseases and conditions.

> **EXODUS 34:6-7**
> AND THE LORD PASSED BEFORE HIM AND PROCLAIMED, "THE LORD, THE LORD GOD, MERCIFUL AND GRACIOUS, LONGSUFFERING, AND ABOUNDING IN GOODNESS AND TRUTH, KEEPING MERCY FOR THOUSANDS, FORGIVING INIQUITY AND TRANSGRESSION AND SIN, BY NO MEANS CLEARING THE GUILTY, VISITING THE INIQUITY OF THE FATHERS UPON THE CHILDREN AND THE CHILDREN'S CHILDREN TO THE THIRD

HOW CAN ONE RECOGNIZE THAT A PERSON MAY BE UNDER A CURSE?

THE INTERVIEW PROCESS

The probable existence of a curse can often be recognized when the person is being interviewed preparatory to prayer for healing or for deliverance ministry. For example, sometimes the person receiving ministry knows he has been cursed and can identify the person who placed the curse on him, when it happened and the curse itself. For example, if a curse was invoked in the course of a violent quarrel, the person may remember it.

Sometimes the person who placed the curse or procured it, tells the cursed person in order to torment him.

The interview may reveal that the person or a family member has been involved in occult practices, rituals or in an occult organization, in a secret society or has made a satanic contract. Such involvement is a common origin point for curses.

Membership in a secret society such as a Masonic organization, by itself, is an indication that a curse may be present.

The interview may reveal that the person receiving ministry has had difficult relationships with various authority figures in his life; parents, teachers, military officers, police, employers, etc. It may reveal that some of these authority figures spoke unintentional curses into his life through derogatory statements. Or it may reveal that the person receiving ministry has imposed some imprecations upon himself.

OBSERVATION

Sometimes a curse can be recognized by the existence of certain conditions apart from any specific pronouncements that can be identified. Derek Prince lists the following conditions which, when two or more are present, are likely indications of a curse[4]:

> Mental or emotional breakdown.
> Repeated or chronic sickness, especially if hereditary.

[4] Prince, _Blessing or Curse, You can Choose!_, Chosen Books, Fleming Revell Co., Old Tappan, NJ, 1990, p. 45.

Barrenness; a tendency to miscarry; menstrual problems.

Breakdown of marriage and family alienation.

Continuing financial insufficiency.

Accident proneness.

A history of suicides, early deaths, or unnatural deaths in the family.

A combination of such conditions should lead the minister to suspect that a curse is present, even if the person receiving ministry cannot recall receiving any curse.

Difficulty in receiving prayer for the presence of the Holy Spirit is an accurate indication of the presence of a curse or of a demonic spirit.

Lack of progress when praying for healing is an indication that inquiry should be made concerning the possible existence of a curse.

Note: It should always be considered that the person under a curse may also have become oppressed by a demonic spirit. This is especially important if the person himself is a former member of a secret society, a Masonic organization or a Satanic cult. In such cases the person will generally need deliverance ministry as well as the breaking of the curse or curses involved.

HOW DO YOU BREAK A CURSE?

The power and authority to break curses comes from the cross and the name of Jesus. Jesus' blood that was shed on the cross is effective for many things besides forgiveness of sin. Also, in the Atonement is the power for healing, power for deliverance, sanctification and the power to break curses. In his letter to the Galatians Paul observed:

> **GALATIANS 3:13-14**
> CHRIST HAS REDEEMED US FROM THE CURSE OF THE LAW, HAVING BECOME A CURSE FOR US (FOR IT IS WRITTEN, "CURSED IS EVERYONE WHO HANGS ON A TREE." THAT THE BLESSING OF ABRAHAM MIGHT COME UPON THE GENTILES IN CHRIST JESUS, THAT WE MIGHT RECEIVE THE PROMISE OF THE SPIRIT THROUGH FAITH. (GAL. 3:13-14.)

As in salvation, healing and deliverance, breaking the bondage of a curse often involves the ministry of a third person. However, a curse can be broken in the name of Jesus by the person who is under it.

The person who has been cursed is most likely to get relief if he cleanses himself spiritually before seeking release. He should:

Repent of all rebellion and sin in his life.

Ask and claim forgiveness for all his sins.

Forgive everyone who has injured him.

Renounce all contact with anything occult or satanic.

Then he may pray for the breaking of all curses and healing of any inner wounds resulting from the curses and receive in faith what he has asked for.[5]

BREAKING A SPECIFIC CURSE

It may be clear from the circumstances and from the person's recollection, that a specific statement of the father or some other authority figure has festered in the son's mind and spirit. For example, a statement by the father that the son would "never amount to anything." Such a curse can be broken by a specific prayer referring to it, such as:

In the name of Jesus, I break the curse over Joe's life resulting from his father's statement that Joe would never amount to anything. I break the power of those words over Joe, in the name of Jesus. In the name of Jesus I break any bondage of those words over Joe.

This should be followed by prayer for healing of any damage to Joe's spirit or emotions caused by the derogatory words spoken to him.

A similar prayer can be made in the case of a witch's hex or other known imprecation specifically mentioning each separate curse known to have been pronounced.

A GENERAL PRAYER BREAKING SEVERAL CURSES

A father or other authority figure may often have given way to exasperation or exaggeration and may have made many derogatory statements about the person receiving ministry – too many to remember. Where details of such statements cannot be remembered, a more general prayer would be appropriate, such as:

> In the name of Jesus, I break every curse on Joe resulting from his father's careless statements about his lack of ability, his lack of intelligence and his limited future possibilities. I break their power over Joe in the name of Jesus. In the name of Jesus I break the bondage of any such words over Joe's life. In the name of Jesus, I pray for the healing of all wounds in Joe resulting from these curses.

If other persons in Joe's life made such statements, such as a teacher, an army officer, a close friend, etc., the power of those statements should also be broken in the name of Jesus.

BREAKING A SELF-IMPOSED CURSE OR ONE RESULTING FROM ONE'S CONDUCT

In cases involving one's own conduct, such as making a careless statement or making a satanic contract, the person should go through the preparatory steps mentioned above from Derek Prince. Then he should address the following items.

> The careless statement must be renounced.
>
> Any vow not to engage in certain conduct must be renounced.
>
> Any vow to the secret society or Satanic society must be renounced.
>
> Membership in the secret society or in the occult organization must be renounced.
>
> The curse pronounced on one's self must be renounced.
>
> The satanic vow and/or contract must be renounced.
>
> If ancestral iniquity is involved, it must be repented of.

[5]*Prince, op. cit., chapter 18.*

Each step should be taken in the name of Jesus.

Then the person under the curse must repent of his own conduct and ask and receive the Lord's forgiveness. After he has done this, the minister can break the power of the curse in the name of Jesus.

The person freed from a curse should destroy any mementos or symbols in his possession of the society or cult or activity that caused the curse, such as jewelry (rings, earrings, cuff links, bracelets, etc.) paper weights, plaques, certificates, uniforms, T-shirts, etc.

Tokens or symbols of any occult activity, if retained, can continue to have an oppressive, demonic power over the person and even over others living or working in the same environment. See the "Special Note About Freemasonry" at the end of this chapter.

FAMILY MEMBERS

Occult activity and membership in occult organizations such as the Masons, can affect family members who have had no contact with the organization on their own. Such family members should renounce the organization, renounce any vows or contracts made by the ancestor or relative. Then the curse should be broken in the name of Jesus.

For members of the family of a Freemason, a renunciation and prayer along the following lines may suffice:

> In the name of Jesus, I renounce every oath taken and the curses and the related penalties pronounced by any ancestor or other relative of mine in any ritual of Freemasonry. I renounce every god honored and every password used in any degree and every spirit causing any illness or disease, in the name of Jesus. I renounce every death wish and every symbolic ritual such as burial and resurrection, in the name of Jesus. Father, I ask you to wash me clean of all uncleanness connected with Freemasonry and to free me from any bondage to fear or any emotional or occultic influence from Freemasonry. In the name of Jesus I break the power over me of any unclean spirit related to Freemasonry.

If the person receiving ministry can remember particular oaths or curses that seem to have an untoward effect on him, they should be added to the list of those renounced and broken.

BREAKING GENERATIONAL CURSES

As noted above, some curses flow from one generation to the next. Often family members are afflicted with the same problems that their ancestors had, such as proneness to illness, proneness to accidents, poverty or addiction. These generational ties can be broken by the person ministering or by the person receiving ministry, through prayer in the name of Jesus as suggested above.

CURSES I PRONOUNCE ON MYSELF

It should be apparent from the preceding discussion that the pronouncement of curses upon anyone is sin. If anyone doubts, the words of the Lord are clear:

> **LUKE 6:27-28**
> LOVE YOUR ENEMIES, DO GOOD TO THOSE WHO HATE YOU, BLESS THOSE WHO CURSE YOU, AND PRAY FOR THOSE WHO SPITEFULLY USE YOU.

And also the words of Paul:

> **ROMANS 12:14**
> BLESS THOSE WHO PERSECUTE YOU; BLESS AND DO NOT CURSE.

If any curse has been pronounced by a believer, he must repent of this conduct and ask God's forgiveness as for any other sin. In addition, he should pronounce a blessing on the ones he cursed, to replace the curse and pray for any necessary healing and restoration for the cursed one.

Also, the believer should be wary of unintended curses caused by careless remarks about another. These also should be repented of and blessing substituted. If anyone feels these unintended curses are not important, he should consider these remarks of the Lord:

> **MATTHEW 12:35-37**
> A GOOD MAN OUT OF THE GOOD TREASURE OF HIS HEART BRINGS FORTH GOOD THINGS, AND AN EVIL MAN OUT OF THE EVIL TREASURE BRINGS FORTH EVIL THINGS. BUT I SAY TO YOU THAT FOR EVERY IDLE WORD MEN MAY SPEAK, THEY WILL GIVE ACCOUNT OF IT IN THE DAY OF JUDGMENT. FOR BY YOUR WORDS YOU WILL BE JUSTIFIED, AND BY YOUR WORDS YOU WILL BE CONDEMNED.

It is easy for someone to fall into the habit of making derogatory statements about others and thus to fall into the error of placing unintended curses upon others. Wisdom suggests that special efforts should be made to break any such dangerous habit.

A SPECIAL NOTE ABOUT FREEMASONRY:

Freemasonry as practiced in the United States is a secret society that has its origins in an effort begun in England to form a universal religion – one in which members of any faith could feel at home in worship and in fellowship with each other.

Not only was Freemasonry started as a religion, but it is practiced as a religion. Among other things, Masonic buildings are called "temples". They contain many religious items and symbols, including thrones, holy books and altars. Its rituals include many elements of various religions all considered equally godly. The Freemasonry "god" is a combination of Jehovah,

Baal and Osiris, though this is not disclosed to members until they are somewhat advanced in the society.

There are devices in Freemasonry designed to make various Masonic rituals appear to be Christian. The Bible is accepted as a holy book – though only as one of several. Many prayers similar to those set out in the New Testament are used in rituals though all references to Jesus are excised from them. A number of rituals use symbolism from the New Testament, including symbolic death, burial and resurrection. But the Christian notions of the Atonement are denied. Jesus' divinity is denied. Since the true God, the Hebrew God, is not worshipped or honored, these practices are deceptive.

The Masonic view of Satan and God is worse than deceptive. That there is a war between Lucifer and the Hebrew God is recognized in the advanced degrees, but there is a grievous twisting of the Christian view of this conflict. Lucifer is considered as beneficent and the Hebrew God as evil. Accordingly, Freemasonry is clearly occultic, blasphemous and demonic.

A Mason progresses through the society by taking the ritual and vows for successive "degrees". Each degree has its ritual and the Mason must in each degree make a vow of secrecy to not disclose any steps of the ritual or of the accompanying vows. He places upon himself, should he break his vow of secrecy, curses of vicious punishment involving death and the destruction of his body in terrible ways.

Freemasonry fell into disrepute in the United States in the 1800s with the death of a popular military officer who disavowed Freemasonry. It was widely considered that he was murdered by his fellow Masons for having breached his vows of secrecy. This disfavor was eventually followed by efforts of the society to re-make its image in various ways. Perhaps most notable was the establishment of Shriners' hospitals in which needy children can receive free medical care.

As a result of these efforts, Freemasonry is now sometimes viewed as a benevolent civic and social society, partly because of the organized fellowship and care for one another and because of the Shriners' hospitals. However, it is actually a deceptive religious organization and blasphemous in its origin and practice.

Probably all secret societies should be avoided by the Christian. However, Freemasonry seems to be particularly malignant in affecting the physical and emotional lives of members and their families. The curses members are required to pronounce upon themselves seem to affect Masons and members of their extended families strongly in adverse ways, even if the Mason keeps his vows.

It seems that fairly often healing, deliverance or receiving the baptism in the Holy Spirit does not occur, for former members or for relatives of members, until the oaths, curses and demonic rituals of Freemasonry are renounced and the curses broken.

Some experienced ministries prefer to break the specific curses of the various Masonic degrees over former members by using specific renunciations and prayers tailored to the specific degree.[6] Anyone ministering to former Masons or members of the families of Masons should consider obtaining a source of such help for example, for use in aiding in the renunciation of the gods, oaths, curses, penalties, passwords, secret signs, rituals, and symbols of the society (See footnote 6).

[6]*See Cassada, op. cit., chapter six, pp. 43-56. For even more detailed renunciations, see Wagner, How to Cast Out Demons, Renew Books, Ventura, CA, 2000, Appendix 5, pp.209-230.*

Chapter 11
DELIVERANCE

OVERVIEW

For years, Pablo Bottari supervised the deliverance tent at Carlos Anacondia crusades in Argentina. There he supervised deliverance ministry to many thousands and personally participated in the deliverance of many hundreds of people, mostly believers. He felt that the deliverance ministry he saw at first was noisy, difficult, lengthy and often humiliating to the person being ministered to. He developed a ten-step model for deliverance which is quiet and effective. The model discussed in this manual is based on his.

DELIVERANCE

"Deliverance" is setting a person free from the oppression of a demonic spirit.

Demons are evil spirits without bodies, under Satan's authority, who seek to harass people and if possible, to move into them. They are restless if they cannot move into a human being (See Matthew 12:43-45). When given such an opportunity, a demonic spirit torments or manipulates the host person in various ways. Understanding demonic spirits and deliverance is of great importance to the church because of the adverse effect such spirits can have on believers, on church unity and on evangelism.

The term "oppression" is used in this manual, rather than "possession" because "possession" implies ownership and complete control. Since a believer has been purchased by the Lord Jesus Christ he cannot be possessed by Satan or his emissary. However, many believers have been host to demonic presences in their years before conversion and these evil spirits do not always leave when their host is converted.

THE EFFECT OF DEMONIC OPPRESSION

A demon may torment the host person with such problems as nightmares, unreasonable fear, general accusations of worthlessness or guilt, shame, pain, illness, depression, irrational behavior, and the like. Some of the symptoms mentioned in this and the following paragraphs of course can have causes other than demonic oppression. Frequently, however, they are caused or augmented by demonic oppression. It can give its host unwelcome and sometimes apparently uncontrollable desire to sin in a particular way, such as a spirit of adultery, of pornography, of anger or of addiction, as examples.

See Acts 5:3 where Peter asks Ananias, a believer:

> **ACTS 5:3**
> **"WHY HAS SATAN FILLED YOUR HEART TO LIE TO THE HOLY SPIRIT …?"**

And Luke reports an event at the Last Supper:

> **LUKE 22:3-4**
> **THEN SATAN ENTERED JUDAS, SURNAMED ISCARIOT, WHO WAS NUMBERED AMONG THE TWELVE. SO HE WENT HIS WAY AND CONFERRED WITH THE CHIEF PRIESTS AND CAPTAINS, HOW HE MIGHT BETRAY HIM TO THEM.**

A demon can push the host person repeatedly into sins and habits he resists and wishes to be free from, and thus be a major cause of disaffection and backsliding. After cycles of committing a particular sin, repenting, being forgiven, resisting, sinning again, repenting, being forgiven, resisting, and sinning again, the believer may become discouraged and leave the church. Or he may live a life of quiet desperation in the church, not realizing he can be free from such oppression.

Demonic oppression is an enemy of evangelizing as it prevents the Christian from achieving victory over certain sins, habits or problems. Demonic oppression impairs his testimony as to the power of Jesus to change lives.

Demonic spirits sometimes cause disease and sometimes impede or prevent healing of injuries and disease. Jesus cast out spirits of deafness, dumbness and epilepsy, among others.

Demonic spirits can carry a weight of spiritual and emotional oppression which dulls spiritual perception and in severe cases, can cause depression. See the reference in Isaiah 61:3 to "the spirit of heaviness."

A demon may work steadily in the host person or it may remain quiet, perhaps for years. The demon may work strongly in him at a later time, perhaps after the host person has achieved a position of spiritual responsibility and status.

The remedy for demonic oppression is deliverance. Deliverance has always been a sign to unbelievers of the power of God over Satan. In contrast to prayer for physical healing, which sometimes does not result in immediate healing, the deliverance ministry is almost always effective when the person receiving ministry is born again and truly desires to be set free.

DELIVERANCE IN NORTH AMERICAN CHURCHES

Demonic oppression has largely been ignored in North American churches. As to unbelievers, this is partly due to the conviction of many that belief in demons is mere superstition and partly because unbelievers are not likely to seek deliverance help or to be accepted for such ministry if they do seek help.

Also, the church has largely ignored demonic oppression among its members, partly due to the theology of some that a true believer cannot be oppressed by demonic spirits. Therefore, all evil spirits leave a new believer at the time of his conversion. Partly due to the noisy, unpleasant and often humiliating method of deliverance commonly used until recent years.

The long-standing indifference of the western church to demonic oppression or "demonization" is changing. The theology that a demon cannot reside in a true believer is giving way as a result of teaching and experience. More books on the subject of deliverance are appearing in Christian bookstores and the number of conferences devoted to the subject and the attendance at such conferences, is increasing. For example, a conference on deliverance held in 2000 drew a capacity audience of several thousand attendees. Churches are discovering that deliverance can be effective in helping new believers achieve a mature lifestyle and in restoring believers to useful service or releasing them into more useful service. As one person who had been a faithful servant in the church for years put it, "I had no idea one could be so free this side of heaven."

As to the method of deliverance, as noted in footnote 1, a ten-step method along the lines advocated by Pablo Bottari is recommended in these notes. It is quiet, pastoral, loving, non-humiliating and very effective. It is followed in all Randy Clark crusades and in many churches.

DELIVERANCE WAS CENTRAL TO THE MINISTRY OF JESUS

In many places where the gospels speak about the ministry of Jesus, deliverance is mentioned. The first chapter of Mark is one example:

> **MARK 1:32-33**
> NOW AT EVENING, WHEN THE SUN HAD SET, THEY BROUGHT TO HIM ALL WHO WERE SICK AND THOSE WHO WERE DEMON-POSSESSED. AND THE WHOLE CITY (CAPERNAUM) WAS GATHERED TOGETHER AT THE DOOR. THEN HE HEALED MANY WHO WERE SICK WITH VARIOUS DISEASES, AND CAST OUT MANY DEMONS; ...
>
> **MARK 1:39**
> AND HE WAS PREACHING IN THEIR SYNAGOGUES THROUGHOUT ALL GALILEE, AND CASTING OUT DEMONS.

Deliverance was also part of Jesus' assignment to the twelve and to the seventy of his followers whom He sent out. In Matthew 10, speaking to the twelve, Jesus said:

> **MARK 10:7-8**
> AND AS YOU GO, PREACH, SAYING, "THE KINGDOM OF HEAVEN IS AT HAND." HEAL THE SICK, CLEANSE THE LEPERS, RAISE THE DEAD, CAST OUT DEMONS. FREELY YOU HAVE RECEIVED, FREELY GIVE.

In Luke 10, speaking of the seventy, Luke records:

> **LUKE 10:17**
> THEN THE SEVENTY RETURNED WITH JOY, SAYING, "LORD, EVEN THE DEMONS ARE SUBJECT TO US IN YOUR NAME."

Deliverance is part of the great commission assigned now to all believers:

> **MARK 16:15-17**
> AND HE SAID TO THEM, "GO INTO ALL THE WORLD AND PREACH THE GOSPEL TO EVERY CREATURE. HE WHO BELIEVES AND IS BAPTIZED WILL BE SAVED; BUT HE WHO DOES NOT BELIEVE WILL BE CONDEMNED. AND THESE SIGNS WILL FOLLOW THOSE WHO BELIEVE: IN MY NAME THEY WILL CAST OUT DEMONS;..."

Casting out demons in the name of Jesus is for "those who believe," which includes all believers!

OCCASIONS FOR MINISTERING DELIVERANCE

CRUSADE SETTINGS

In a crusade setting, the speaker may preach on freedom from bondages and may pray strongly for people in the audience to be released from bondages. During such prayers demons in some of the group being prayed for may manifest, causing them to shake or tremble, to perspire, to fall or perhaps to scream. These people need to be quieted if necessary and assisted to a quiet prayer room for ministry.

WORSHIP SETTINGS

Powerful worship can stir up demons. Manifestations can be provoked in an individual during worship or prayer time in a church or small group.

PRIVATE SETTINGS

Perhaps more often, a Christian may seek help in a private setting for a spiritual or emotional problem such as depression, unreasonable fear, an inability to break an embarrassing and unwanted habit, or some other symptom without any outward manifestation.

WHEN MINISTERING TO THE SICK

It frequently happens that spiritual blockages are encountered when ministering to a sick person. Encountering an afflicting spirit, a spirit of pain or a spirit of the particular disease such as cancer is common.

Accordingly, you may have occasion to minister deliverance to some who exhibit visible manifestations and probably more often, to individuals where no demonic manifestation is occurring when your ministry begins. Often, in the latter type of case, no strong outward manifestation occurs at all during the ministry.

DISTINGUISHING DEMONIC FROM HOLY SPIRIT MANIFESTATIONS

If a manifestation begins when a speaker or a ministry team member is praying powerfully against demonic oppression, the manifestation can be assumed to be due to a demonic presence. Conversely, if a manifestation begins when a speaker or a ministry team member is praying for a blessing, for guidance or for impartation of a spiritual gift, the manifestation is probably due to the working of the Holy Spirit.

There may be occasions in personal ministry when the circumstances don't indicate whether a physical manifestation is the effect of the Holy Spirit or whether a demon is manifesting. Some clues are:

If the person is harming himself or others, biting, scratching, etc., a demonic manifestation is indicated.

The physical appearance of the prayee may betray a demonic presence. Such signs include severe bodily contortions, facial contortions, sudden or unusual changes in voice, refusal to make eye contact, eyes rolled back so that only the whites are visible, screaming, or hostile demeanor or behavior.

Other clues suggesting a demonic presence are:

> Sudden headache
>
> Nausea
>
> Sudden violent actions
>
> Destructive actions, such as kicking or breaking furniture
>
> Hissing
>
> Claw-like motions
>
> Atypical foul language

However, if a manifestation begins when one is ministering to an oppressed person, it can be a sign that the Holy Spirit is at work in the person's body. Such manifestations are usually (though not always) minor, such as feeling heat, tingling or electricity somewhere in the body, fluttering eyelids, trembling or shaking, falling to the floor and remaining there peacefully, or sometimes laughter.

In doubtful situations, one can ask the person how he feels, whether he feels good or bad. If he feels at peace or that the Lord is speaking to him, the Holy Spirit is probably at work. If he feels terrified or hopeless or under spiritual attack, or if he does not answer in his own voice, it is likely a demonic manifestation.

The gift of discerning of spirits and the leading of the Holy Spirit are valuable aids at such times. Pray for the gift and always ask the Holy Spirit to be present and for His leading.

YOUR PERSONAL PREPARATION

Pablo Bottari emphasizes several things for those who would be involved in a deliverance ministry. He comments:

Above all, this ministry should be one of love. Behind all deliverance should be God's heart of love for a suffering soul. Pray daily for grace to receive more of God's love and to be a channel for His love to others. When ministry occurs, pray especially for His love toward those to whom you will minister. The primary object of ministry is not to punish a demon. It is to help a person God loves.

Order is important. Demons respect authority. If another dilutes the authority of the person leading in the ministry by assuming some authority to himself, he makes it harder for the leader to deal successfully with the demon involved.

Those ministering should recognize some limitations to a deliverance ministry. It is useless to expel a demon against the oppressed person's will. If the person is unwilling to change their lifestyle that cause the oppression or renounce the agreement made with Satan specifically and audibly, deliverance is futile.

Under such circumstances, the demon will return, perhaps bringing others with it. See Matthew 12:43-45, where Jesus expressly speaks of demons returning to dwell again in the person from whom they have been expelled.

The minister[1] should keep in mind that a demon cannot oppress a person unless some avenue of access has been opened to it by unforgiveness, hate, abuse, sin, unclean sex, illness, trauma, or some other circumstance. We call such avenues of access "open doors".

Demons are very legalistic, typically refusing to leave a person unless their avenues of entrance are renounced by the host person. The objective of a deliverance ministry accordingly is two-fold: 1) to expel or drive away any demon; and 2) to close its avenue of access and enable the victim to keep the avenue of access closed in the future in order to prevent any return of the evil spirit.

[3]In these notes, the term "minister" refers to the person helping the prayee to get free.

In addition to the above, the minister should review the suggestions for personal preparation set out in the sections of this manual on Protocol, Prayer Guidelines and Healing. They apply equally to preparation for ministering deliverance.

WHEN COMMENCING MINISTRY

Be sure to ask the Holy Spirit to be present and assist you before you begin to minister. The Holy Spirit greatly desires to assist you to help the person to whom you are ministering. Ask for His help and wait for His leading at every step of the way. He <u>will</u> help you!

Remember that the prayee[2] probably is a hurting person. He may have endured severe verbal or physical abuse, trauma, disappointment, grief, satanic rituals, or a long illness. You may see some or much weeping. Don't hesitate to interrupt the ten-step model to pray for the healing of his wounds and hurts. You may want to do this more than once during the ministry.

It is often most effective to work in a team of two or three with one person taking the lead and the others supporting him with prayer, discernment, note-taking, etc. However, to avoid diluting the leader's authority, the supporters generally should not speak directly to the prayee or touch him, but should communicate with the leader by way of a note or in a quiet voice. The leader makes the decision as to what to do with the suggestion or the discernment of the supporter. In a long ministry time, members of the team may trade places passing leadership from one to another.

The caution about more than one person touching the prayee does not apply during times of praying for the healing of inner wounds and hurts. At such times, the possible dilution of the leader's authority is not a problem.

A TEN-STEP MODEL FOR PRAYING FOR DELIVERANCE

The following ten steps are followed in a session where the minister does not know the host person well, such as in most cases in a crusade or other public meeting setting. In some settings, some of these steps might be omitted. For example, where the minister knows the prayee is a believer and really wants to be set free, steps 4 and 5 would be omitted. If there is no manifestation during the ministry, step 2 and probably step 3 would be omitted.

STEP 1: GIVE THE INDIVIDUAL PRIORITY

Keep a loving attitude, not a militant attitude. Firmness is necessary in casting out a demon, but in the meantime, the prayee needs to feel loved and accepted.

Be encouraging. Raise hope. Emphasize to the prayee that Jesus can set him free. Don't emphasize the power of the demon. It is subject to you in the name of Jesus. Remember that the prayee may have been in bondage for years and perhaps he has received many prayers that were not completely effective. He may have lost hope of being set free. To build up his hope will help in the ministry.

[2] In these notes, the term "prayee" or the term "host person" is sometimes used to refer to the person receiving ministry.

STEP 2: IF A SPIRIT IS MANIFESTING OR IF ONE MANIFESTS DURING YOUR MINISTRY, MAKE THE SPIRIT BE QUIET AND SUBMIT TO YOU IN THE NAME OF JESUS

Take authority over the spirit. Tell it, "Submit, in the name of Jesus!" or "Be quiet, in Jesus' name!" or similar commands. Repeat such commands until the spirit is quiet. If you think the prayee is aware of what is going on, you may want to tell him you are talking to the spirit that is manifesting and not to him.

Don't be surprised if this takes time. Be persistent. You may have to command the spirit several times – or even many times -- to submit. However, it will come under submission.

If others gather while you are quieting the spirit, ask them not to touch the prayee and not to speak or pray loudly. Touching or speaking to the prayee, or loud praying, tends to keep the spirit stirred up. Your objective is not to keep the spirit stirred up. It is to get the spirit to be quiet so you can talk to the prayee.[3]

STEP 3: ESTABLISH AND MAINTAIN COMMUNICATION WITH THE PRAYEE

You must be able to talk with the person receiving ministry because you must have his cooperation if the deliverance is to be successful. He cannot cooperate while a spirit is manifesting. If he cannot cooperate or if he does not want to cooperate, he will soon be oppressed again even if the deliverance seems to be successful.

If you are not sure the prayee can hear you, ask him if he can, whether or not his eyes are closed.

If you are not in a quiet place, tell the prayee, when he can hear you, that you want to go to a quiet place. If he is lying down, or seated, or on the floor, tell him to take control of his body and stand up. Just say, "Take control of your body now and stand up. I'll help you to a quiet place where we can pray" or the equivalent. He will be able to stand and walk though he may need some help. The spirits may manifest again on the way to the prayer room and may have to be brought under submission again.

Don't start to minister until you are settled in the prayer room. If you try to minister on the way, the spirit is likely to manifest again. Speak quietly to the prayee. Encourage him. Tell him he is doing fine. Be calm and loving.

Maintaining communication may require additional commands to the spirit to submit during ministry. The prayee may drop his head, he may close his eyes or his eyes may wander. Ask him to hold his head up, to open his eyes and to look at you. If you are in doubt as to whether he can hear you, ask him if he can.

[3]Pablo Bottari mentions a revealing case: His wife had quieted a manifesting spirit in a young woman when a very loving pastor came by who wished to contribute to the event. With the best of intentions, he touched the young woman and said to her: "Be calm, everything is going to be okay." The spirit in her immediately started to scream again.

If he cannot do these things, a spirit is involved and you then order the spirit to submit.

If the prayee gets up and moves around, take authority over the spirit out loud and tell the prayee to come back and sit down.

A spirit in the prayee may speak to you or growl or whine. It may threaten you, argue with you, give you orders, and ask questions. It may cause the person to make faces at you or to make clawing motions with his hands. Don't speak to it except to order it to be quiet in the name of Jesus.

Maintaining communication can be time-consuming if it must be repeated. However, it is absolutely necessary. Unless you are in communication with the person, you won't have his cooperation and the ministry will not be successful.

Some difficulty may be encountered if the spirit speaks to you in the voice of the person. You may have to determine whether a spirit or the person is speaking by the nature of the talk. If it is arguing, questioning, uncooperative, you can assume that it is a spirit.

Try to be in an environment without noise or other distractions. If bystanders or co-workers loudly pray in tongues or give independent commands to the spirit or speak to the prayee, it will make your ministry more difficult. It tends to erode your authority and may cause the spirit or spirits to manifest or to make the prayee resist ministry. Ministry is easier if only one person touches or talks to the person, except during times of prayer for healing.

STEP 4: ASK THE PRAYEE WHAT HE WANTS TO BE FREE FROM AND TRY TO MAKE SURE HE ACTUALLY WANTS TO GET FREE

In a crusade situation, ask the person receiving ministry what he wants to be freed from. If he is uncertain, ask him what the speaker was praying about when the spirit in him started to manifest. Other helpful initial questions are whether he is trying to break any habit without success or whether he has any conduct he considers odd or weird.

In a private ministry, the prayee probably will know what bondages he wants to be set free from. This can include one or two specific bondages or it may involve a broader ministry – a thorough housecleaning. The prayee may have communicated this information in advance to the person who will be ministering to him.

If the prayee indicates that he does not want ministry even though a spirit has manifested, abide by his decision. If he wants to leave after partial ministry, allow him to leave. Or you may encounter attitudes that indicate lack of desire for complete freedom. Do not try to detain the prayee or to minister to him against his will.

Some wish to be free from the compulsive element of a bad habit, such as smoking or anger or pornography, but don't want to give up the activity. Dabbling in the conduct that opened the door will open it again and the compulsive element – the bondage – will return.

Some don't think evil spirits exist, but want "some help." Or a person may ask for deliverance "just in case" a spirit is present, but without any conviction that help is needed or any intent to change his lifestyle. Or a person may want deliverance from one bondage, but not from another.

Some who exhibit what seems to be a demonic manifestation will insist that the manifestation is the activity of the Holy Spirit.

Some ask for ministry primarily to get attention and sympathy.

Unless God sovereignly intervenes, it is probably not possible to permanently deliver a person from bondage unless he recognizes that it is caused by a spirit and genuinely desires to be set free. Sincere repentance and renunciation of the conduct or attitude and the spirit involved are essential. Without these, the prayee is likely to be in bondage again soon even if the deliverance apparently is successful.

If after discussion, you find that the prayee doesn't want deliverance, wants to continue his present lifestyle anyway or is not a candidate for deliverance for some other reason, pray for him and bless him. But don't pray for his deliverance. Encourage him to come back later for deliverance help if he wishes to do so. Don't be offended. Be loving and kind.

STEP 5: MAKE SURE THE PRAYEE HAS ACCEPTED JESUS AS HIS SAVIOR AND LORD

The ministry recipient will need the help of the Holy Spirit to stay free. If he is not a Christian, he probably will be back in bondage shortly even if he is delivered. This should be explained to him. It isn't wise to try to deliver him in the hope that he will become a believer as a result of getting free.

Perhaps you can lead him to Christ. If you can't, pray for him. Bless him. Pray for the healing of his hurts and wounds. Let him know by your attitude that you are not offended. Be loving. But don't cast out any spirits. Explain why you don't—because he won't be able to stay free. Encourage him to take the step of making Jesus his Lord and then return for deliverance.

If the person is a young Christian, it is extremely important for him to be in or to get into a support group such as a house group, a cell group, or to have a strong supportive person who will take responsibility for helping him.

MINISTRY STEPS

Go on to these steps only if you feel that the prayee really wants to get free, and only if he is a believer.

STEP 6: INTERVIEW THE PRAYEE TO DISCOVER THE EVENT OR EVENTS, OR THE RELATIONSHIP SITUATIONS THAT HAVE LED TO HIS BONDAGE OR BONDAGES

In the interview, look for the "open doors" that have given entrance to the spirit or spirits. Look for causes. Start with possible causes of the particular bondage the person wants to be free from. If there is no obvious other place to start, begin with his relationship with his father and with his mother. Then continue on through other relationships. Then through other areas.

Starting with parents is often helpful, because no one has had perfect parents. Problems in this area are often severe. To get free in this area will encourage the prayee. Sometimes discussion in this area reveals other areas where help is needed, such as the breaking of curses, the breaking of inner vows, etc.

Some find it helpful to interview the prayee by areas. Some major areas and associated spirits that may have entered are listed in **Appendix 1** of this manual.

The purpose of the interview is to expose the places where forgiveness is required, where healing is needed and where repentance and breaking of bondages is needed. These places are open doors. For an explanation of closing these doors, see Step 7.

In the relationship areas, look for places where the prayee has been hurt by others and for ways the prayee himself has sinned or taken in spirits through emotions that are not from God. In addition to resentment, anger, etc., he may have taken in fear, despair, rejection, self-pity, and the like. He may have made inner vows as to his future conduct that are now keeping him in bondage.

The most important relationships are likely to be the relationships between the person receiving ministry and his parents. These relationships – or lack of them – are likely to be prolonged, and are likely to have occurred during the person's most formative young years. Questions should be asked that are likely to get at sore points. Some examples might be:

> "What was your father like?"
>
> "Were you close to him?"
>
> "Was he openly loving and affectionate? Did he hug you, tell you he was glad you were in the family?"
>
> "Was he critical of you? How did he show it? Did he make critical remarks to you or about you? What kind of things did he say to you? How did they make you feel?"
>
> "Did he punish you unfairly? Were you afraid of him?"
>
> "Did he support you in school and activities?"
>
> "Was he gone a lot?"
>
> "Did he favor you over the other children? Or vice versa?"
>
> "Did he and your mother fight in your presence? What did they fight about?"
>
> "Are your parents divorced? Did either of them blame you for the divorce?"

Similar questions would be asked about the person's relationship with his mother. Then questions about other significant relationships would follow relating to siblings, teachers, schoolmates, employers, husband or wife.

In the relationship areas, the minister is looking for hurts and for emotional reactions to the hurts. These will be places where doors were open that may have let evil spirits in. Those who have caused hurts will need to be forgiven (see Step 7).

Emotional responses to hurts and disappointments (such as resentment, anger, rejection, self-pity and the like, and even depression) and inner vows (such as, "I'll never be like my father!", or "I will never speak to her again!") are common and very understandable. However these emotions and vows are not from God and will need to be repented of, forgiveness asked, vows broken and the doors closed.

After interviewing the person about relationships, the minister can proceed with closing doors in those areas before going on (See step 7). Or he can go on to other areas and wait to close all open doors at the same time.

After dealing with relationships with significant people in the prayee's life, the minister moves on to other areas such as the occult, sex outside of marriage, persistent sin in some area, a long illness, drugs, and the like, where he looks simply for participation (not necessarily for places where the host person has been hurt, as in the relationship areas). In these areas simple participation, sometimes merely participation of someone in his family, can be an open door for oppression by evil spirits.

In a crusade setting, the important area will generally be the area being prayed for by the speaker when the manifestation began. In a private setting, the prayee more likely will already have in mind the particular bondage or bondages troubling him (although he may not attribute them to demonic oppression).

The possibility of a curse should be considered if the prayee has persistent difficulty in an aspect of his life, such as inability to keep a job, being accident prone, barrenness, sense of worthlessness, repeated illness, etc. Curses can arise from occult practices such as Satanic rituals or pacts with Satan, his membership or membership of a family member in Freemasonry or other false religion, careless words spoken by someone in authority over him (such as, "You never do anything right!," "You'll never be a success!," "You are just like your mother!") or by himself (such as, "I'd like to die!," "I felt so ashamed.")

The more thorough the interview process is (and the more detailed the forgiveness and repentance are in step 7) the better. This is especially important where depression, self-mutilation, rejection, shame, guilt, self-condemnation, loneliness, etc. are involved.

An alternative structure for conducting an interview, using the areas of "body," "soul" and "spirit," is set out in **Appendix 2**. The questioning process under either approach is very much the same.

SOME TIPS ABOUT INTERVIEWING

It is more likely to refresh the prayee's recollection to ask him about hurts than about the need to forgive. "Did your father hurt your feelings in any way?" is more likely to get a meaningful response than "Do you need to forgive your father for anything?"

Freemasonry and occult activities can affect the prayee whether he personally was involved or any member of his family. Even if the activity was short-lived or perhaps just for fun.

Fear is an entry point for many different spirits and a problem in many illnesses.

If there are many spirits, it helps for one of the team to make a list of them as the interview progresses so that the prayee can renounce each of them by name.

Don't be hurried. It is better to have two relaxed sessions than one hurried session.

Don't try to stir up demons, intimidate them, torment them or get them to name themselves. These actions may hurt the prayee and do not help you. Except for keeping demons quiet, ignore them until they are renounced and you expel them.

In some cases, the person being helped cannot remember something you consider important. For example, he may be unable to remember anything about his life between the ages of 8 and 14. In such a case it is okay to interrupt the ministry. Have him go home and ask the Holy Spirit to help him remember anything significant about that time in his life and come back to resume the ministry later. The Holy Spirit will often bring the significant item (in this case, the reason for the blockage of his memory) to his mind.

In steps 6, 7 and 8, as in step 2, it is more effective if only one person speaks to the person being helped and if only the speaker touches him. If others speak to him or touch him, it seems to erode the leader's authority, cause confusion and allow the spirits to manifest or to cause the prayee to stop cooperating with the ministry or even to resist it. If others have thoughts, they should tell them quietly to the one leading the ministry and let him communicate to the prayee when and as he decides.

STEP 7: LEAD THE PRAYEE IN "CLOSING" THESE "DOORS" TO THE ADMISSION OF SPIRITS

"Leading", in this case, usually means having the prayee repeat sentences after you. After some repetitions, he probably can take the steps on his own.

"Closing a door" involves three or four steps depending on the situation. If forgiveness of someone is needed, it involves steps (A) through (D) below. If there is no one to forgive in the circumstances, only steps (B) through (D) are followed.

A: Forgiving the One who Has Caused Hurt or Led Him into the Wrong Conduct

Forgiveness should be specific, item by item. The more specific, the better. Specific forgiveness brings greater release and freedom than general forgiveness does.

Have the prayee forgive specifically every hurt he has mentioned in your interview and every additional hurt the Holy Spirit brings to his mind. The Holy Spirit will often remind him of things he did not mention in the interview process.

Forgiveness should be followed by releasing to God the person who caused the hurt -- to let him be as he is and blessing him. Releasing the person who has hurt the prayee should include a commitment to take the prayee's hands off the person and stop trying to change him—to leave changes up to God. This is very important. Sometimes it is very difficult when spouses are involved! Releasing the person and blessing him will make the forgiveness more solid.

NOTE: Sometimes the prayee has been hurt so deeply that he feels he simply cannot forgive the person who hurt him. Try to lead him into forgiveness. Explain to him that forgiveness is first of all a decision he makes, not a feeling. Explain that if he does not forgive, he will not be forgiven. Using the phrase "I choose to forgive..." may help the prayee step into the forgiving mode. For example, you might lead him in a sentence like: "I choose to forgive Joe for blaming me for the accident when he broke his arm."

If the prayee still cannot forgive, ask him if you can pray for him. If he says yes, quietly bind the spirit of unforgiveness in him and cast it out of him. Then see if he can forgive. Sometimes that breaks the log jam.

However, if the prayee does not come to the place of forgiveness, you should stop the deliverance ministry. Pray for his wounds and hurts to be healed (especially for the hurt that he is hung up on), and ask God's rich blessing on him. But don't go for deliverance with him. Don't be judgmental. Be loving. But explain to him that you cannot help him get free from his bondage until he is ready to forgive each person who has hurt him.

B: Repenting of Each of the Prayee's own Sins in the Situation, Specifically and Asking God's Forgiveness for Them

The prayee may have joined in wrong conduct and may need to repent and ask forgiveness.

The situation or the actions of another person, may have caused bad emotions that seem quite normal from a human standpoint, such as: resentment; anger, hate, murder; anxiety, pride, rejection, etc. These reactions are very understandable and thus may seem excusable. Nonetheless, they are not of God but of the enemy. And they open the door to oppression. For example, if the person has taken in spirits of hate and bitterness he will probably not be able to get relief from them until he repents of letting them in and asks God's forgiveness for doing so.

A prayer of repentance might be:

> "Father, I repent of the resentment, anger and bitterness I have felt toward my friend Amy (or my father, or my employer, etc.) and I repent of having taken in feelings of rejection, loneliness and despair over that situation. I intend to turn away from all such feelings and I ask your forgiveness for them."

Another might be:

> "Dear God, I repent of sharing my body with _____ and _____ (naming each person). I turn away from all fornication and every other unclean sex activity. I purpose to follow your plan for my life. Please forgive me for having had unclean sex with those people. I give back to them any part of their person I have taken from them in these acts, and I take back any part of my own person I have given to them."

C: RENOUNCING THE SPIRITS INVOLVED IN THE NAME OF JESUS

Renunciation should be audible and firm.

Renunciation is not a prayer to God. It is spoken to the spirit involved, who is an enemy. It should be spoken as a command to an enemy and not a petition to God.

Renunciation of spirits should include spirits taken in which may not necessarily have come in through sin of the prayee. For example, if a child witnesses his parents fighting (verbally or physically), he will likely take in spirits of confusion, anxiety, fear, insecurity and others. Spirits taken in without the sin of the prayee need to be renounced the same as those that entered through his wrong attitudes or other fault.

In the case of sex outside marriage, the prayee has almost certainly taken in unclean sex spirits from his partner or partners and should renounce them in general terms.

If the prayee has made any pact with Satan or if he has made an inner vow of some kind or if you believe he is under a curse, such pacts and vows must be renounced and any curse must be broken, in the name of Jesus.

Some examples of renunciation might be:

> "In the name of Jesus I renounce you spirits of rejection, loneliness, despair and hopelessness."
>
> "In the name of Jesus, I renounce the vow I made never to forgive (Joe)."

D: BREAKING THE BONDAGE CAUSED BY THE SIN, THE CONDUCT, THE ATTITUDE, THE SPIRIT, THE VOW, OR THE CURSE, AS INDICATED, IN THE NAME OF JESUS

Usually you will do this (firmly, vigorously) for the person, keeping eye contact with him. If he is participating and sturdy, he can do it for himself.

Insist on eye contact at this point. If the prayee has difficulty keeping eye contact with you, do not try to break the power of spirits and to expel them right away. Wait until the prayee has renounced other spirits and then return to this step.

It can be a help to the prayee for you to state that the door is closed on the spirits renounced so that the spirits, when cast out, cannot return unless he takes them in again. Pablo Bottari suggests a proclamation like this:

> "In Jesus' name I break the power of the spirits of (anger, hate, fornication, and depression) over you, Mary, so that when they are cast out they will not come back."

To break a curse, you as the minister might say firmly:

> "In the name of Jesus, Tom, I break the power of any curse over you from your father's careless words to you, specifically including your father's comment that you can never do anything right, and that you would never amount to anything."

Or:

> "In the name of Jesus, I break every curse placed on you due to your father's Freemasonry[4], and I break every generational curse that has come down to you from any of your ancestors."

PRAYER FOR HEALING

The interview process (step 6) and the door-closing process (step 7) can be extremely painful as the prayee re-lives deep hurts. You may see some weeping or grief. Perhaps deep grief and much weeping. You may want to stop at intervals to ask God to heal his hurts, his broken heart, etc. Don't be afraid to put your arms around him and hold him (man to man, woman to woman) if he weeps or shows other signs of distress. The prayee often needs comfort, hope, loved and protected. He needs to hear that tears are okay and can be part of his healing process. If his distress is profound, it may be helpful to ask Jesus to speak directly to him about it.

Step 7 can be interrupted. If the prayee cannot identify the cause of feelings he has, such as fear, it may be best to adjourn the ministry if time permits and have him ask the Holy Spirit to show him the cause. The Holy Spirit will do this and the ministry can then be taken up again dealing specifically with the revealed cause.

STEP 8: CAST OUT THE UNCLEAN SPIRIT OR (USUALLY) SPIRITS IN THE NAME OF JESUS

Simply cast them out. It is not necessary to send them somewhere.

If the doors have been effectively closed, the spirits will leave quietly and quickly. One or two commands are enough to cast them out. If you find that:

> more than two or three commands are needed, or
>
> a spirit "sticks in the throat" of the prayee, or
>
> the prayee commences to groan or sweat or strain, or
>
> he begins to feel nauseated, or to have a headache,

it is a signal that not all doors have been closed. Go back to the interview stage! Find and close the unclosed doors.

Often the prayee will know what doors have not been closed. You may discover them simply by asking him.

[4]For more detail on Freemasonry, see the special note on Freemasonry beginning in the chapter on Curses.

The prayee may or may not display some manifestation of the spirits' leaving. He may cough, yawn, burp, wince, jerk, etc. Often, the spirits seem to leave as they are renounced and there may be little or no manifestation during the casting-out step. However, the prayee usually will feel free. He may feel lighter. He may feel like laughing or deeply peaceful. If none of these occur, you may not know for a day or so whether the deliverance is successful.

If after step 8 the prayee appears distressed, sullen, etc., or is nauseated, has a headache, he probably is not free and you need to look for more doors to close.

Some judgment may be exercised in performing steps 6, 7, and 8 as to whether to close all open doors before expelling the spirits or whether to close doors and cast them out by groupings.

Probably the ideal method is to close all doors before casting out any demons. This is recommended by Pablo Bottari. His reason for closing all doors before the casting out begins, is that sometimes the spirits that are being cast out may cling to a demon that still has a right to stay in the prayee. This can give rise to the difficulties mentioned above and is a signal that more doors need to be closed.

Some who are experienced in deliverance ministry believe it is effective to cast the demons out by groups. That is, those related to unforgiveness, resentment, anger, etc., can be cast out before dealing with those related to, for example, unclean sex or trauma.

Where numerous spirits in many categories are involved, the minister may choose this route simply because of the difficulty of keeping track of things. If it seems to work well, fine. If it doesn't work well, go back to the Pablo Bottari method.

WHEN YOU THINK YOU HAVE FINISHED STEP 8 ...

When you think you have finished step 8, ask the prayee whether there are other spirits to be dealt with. Often he will know if there is another or others. By this time he is usually freed up enough to be able to participate effectively in his own relief. If something comes to light, deal with it as per steps 6-8.

Next, ask the Holy Spirit to show one of the three or four of you (you, the intercessor, the prayee, and any friend, spouse or parent who is present) whether there are additional spirits to be exposed and expelled. Wait some moments to see if the Holy Spirit shows someone something. If He does, ask the prayee, gently, whether there is a need in the area the Holy Spirit has shown you. Remember that you might hear incorrectly, so be careful not to speak too strongly or accusatory. Again, if something comes to light, deal with it as per steps 6 to 8.

STEP 9: ASK THE PRAYEE TO PRAISE AND THANK JESUS FOR HIS DELIVERANCE

If the prayee cannot thank Jesus or if there is further demonic manifestation when he does, it is a signal that there are more doors to be closed and more spirits to be expelled. Ask the Holy Spirit for His help. Go back to step 6 or 7 as indicated.

STEP 10: ASK THE PRAYEE TO PRAY FOR THE HOLY SPIRIT TO FILL HIM AND FILL ALL THE PLACES FORMERLY OCCUPIED BY THE EVIL SPIRITS

If the prayee cannot say this prayer or if there is further demonic manifestation when he does, this also is a signal that there are more doors to be closed and more spirits to be expelled. Again, ask the Holy Spirit for His help. Go back to step 6 or 7 as indicated.

MINI-DELIVERANCES

DEALING WITH ONLY ONE OR TWO AREAS

If time permits, for people who come off the street or for people who want a full "house-cleaning" or for new believers or for people who are in depression, it is good to consider all of the areas listed in **Appendix 1**.

Sometimes, however, time does not permit a thorough housecleaning, in which case you might deal only with the areas of bondage that are indicated by the manifestations or that are indicated by the prayee's concerns. In such a case, the prayee should be advised that a more thorough deliverance is desirable.

WHEN PRAYING FOR THE SICK

Sometimes when praying for the sick, it will become apparent that the prayee has areas of unforgiveness that need attention. In such cases it often seems appropriate simply to lead the prayee in a very brief time of forgiveness of the person or people involved. Lead him in repentance for his own unforgiveness and to ask forgiveness for his sin. Have him renounce the spirits of anger and unforgiveness, and then you, the minister, break the power of that unforgiveness spirit and cast it out. All this is done quietly and without a lot of interviewing.

Frequently a sick person has an afflicting spirit, a spirit of pain, a spirit of infirmity or stiffness, and the like. These spirits can usually be cast out with a word. If one is praying short prayers with frequent interviewing, he can see the effectiveness of casting out such spirits with a word.

In the case of some sicknesses, such as diabetes, cancer, etc., a strong evil spirit of the sickness may be present. Where this is recognized, the spirit may have to be expelled in a much longer session with finding the open door, closing it, etc.

USE OF A QUESTIONNAIRE

Where it is practicable to use a questionnaire, a questionnaire can greatly reduce the time otherwise spent in interviewing the prayee to find areas where deliverance is needed and in finding the open doors. (Step 6 of the ten-step model.)

The questionnaire can be as thorough as desired. Of course, use of a questionnaire will not be possible in a public setting. But it can be used in private appointment settings where a thorough questionnaire is appropriate and in many cases desirable.

The questionnaire should be answered by the prayee and the answers given to the minister ahead of the ministry session so that the minister can consider the approach he wishes to take in the ministry and whether to seek additional information.

An example of a thorough questionnaire is set out in **Appendix 4**. A more detailed and exhaustive questionnaire can be found in *How to Cast out Demons*, by Doris Wagner.

POST-DELIVERANCE MINISTRY

Your ministry is not complete after you have successfully ministered deliverance to a needy person. His bondages may have been broken, but he may need healing of his emotions, healing of relationships, rest, suggestions on staying free of bondages in the future, counseling, or other help. As a ministry team member or lay minister, you may not be qualified to give counseling to the prayee, but in other areas all of us should be prepared to give him or her significant help. This help should always include prayer.

Also, this help also should always include the caution that the prayee's continued freedom is not automatic, and that he must take steps to preserve it. Help him with suggestions for staying free. (See **Appendix 3** for steps to maintain your freedom.)

GIVE HIM PRACTICAL SUGGESTIONS THAT YOU HAVE FOUND HELPFUL IN YOUR OWN SPIRITUAL WALK

ENCOURAGE THE PRAYEE TO MAINTAIN THE NORMAL PRACTICES FOR A HEALTHY SPIRITUAL LIFE

> Daily quiet time.
> Daily Bible reading.
> Getting into a live Christian fellowship.
> Participating in communion.

ENCOURAGE THE PRAYEE TO CONSIDER WHETHER HIS HABIT PATTERNS NEED TO BE CHANGED

The prayee may have a habit that he must change and it may not change automatically just because he is delivered of demons that were encouraging him in it. Help him to see the importance of changing habit patterns. Each time he finds himself falling into a wrong habit, he must consciously turn away from following that pattern. He can remind himself that the tormenting spirit is gone. He can ask God to help him change his habit. He may have to retrain his mind. It may help him to ask God to give him the mind of Christ – and to give no room to Satan. The prayee may have to consciously work on changing his habits for a few days, weeks or months. He may very well need the help of a group or of a friend. Discuss this with him.

ENCOURAGE THE PRAYEE TO WALK IN FORGIVENESS AS A LIFESTYLE

Explain that forgiveness is a decision, not a feeling and that he can forgive a person even if he doesn't feel like it. He can choose to forgive. His spirit can have the rule over his emotions and it is important to forgive for his own best interest.

EXPLAIN THAT QUICK FORGIVENESS FOR CURRENT HURTS IS IMPORTANT

Perhaps explain that forgiving for past hurts is a bit like an onion -- it comes in layers. He may forgive his father today for everything that the Holy Spirit has shown him. But after a few days or weeks, he thinks of something else his father said that irritated him and he has a desire for revenge or he wishes he had thought of a cutting reply he could have made or the like. These are signs that he needs to forgive his father for this additional item. This process can go on for a long time. He may need to forgive the same person several times for the same hurt.

The prayee needs to know that this forgiveness process – of needing to forgive the same person more than once (sometimes many times) – is normal and not a sign that the deliverance ministry was a failure.

ENCOURAGE THE PRAYEE TO GET INTO A SUPPORT GROUP

This is one of the most important steps the prayee can take. A support group (perhaps a cell group or care group) or person is vitally important. Discuss what help is available in a support group. Tell him how it has benefited you. Suggest where he can find a support group, if he isn't in one. Perhaps he can ask his pastor where to find a good support group.

ENCOURAGE THE PRAYEE TO TAKE ALL CURRENT HURTS QUICKLY TO GOD FOR HEALING

In this life, hurts are sure to come. He need not walk in bondage to them. Encourage him to ask God for healing promptly, each time he realizes that some word or some event has hurt him or hurt his feelings. Suggest that he may have to resist the desire to wallow in the hurt. He may have to resist self-pity.

ENCOURAGE THE PRAYEE THAT HE SHOULD MAKE RESTITUTION IF HE CAN

Encourage the prayee to make restitution to anyone he has defrauded and to apologize to anyone he knows he has offended. This is an important part of staying free. If he does not make restitution or apologize as necessary, these events will be a spiritual burden on him and can help to cause him to slip away from a close walk with the Lord.

CONSIDER OTHER SUGGESTIONS AS TO HOW TO STAY FREE

You might remind him that Satan is not happy about his being delivered and may try especially hard to tempt him back into the old sin to open the door again. Encourage him to resist temptation and give him suggestions as to how he might become more successful in resisting. Some possibilities are:

> Praise God, singing or listening to praise songs, reading Psalms.
>
> Pray in tongues.
>
> Take authority over tempting spirits in the name of Jesus and send them away.
>
> Thank God for setting him free.
>
> If he falls, he can repent quickly and get the door closed again.
>
> If Satan accuses him of being a sinner, he can say: "You're right, Satan. Just look at what Jesus has forgiven me for!"
>
> He can look for ways to remind himself that Jesus is his Lord. You can tell him that a number one priority should be to make Jesus the Lord over every area of his life.
>
> Ask daily for filling with the Holy Spirit.

You might suggest scripture passages that would be helpful to him. Perhaps Galatians 5:1; 1Corinthians 10:13; Philippians 4:6-7.

Use passages that have been helpful to you personally.

Some things you can consider praying for as part of the ministry session:

> Thank God for setting the prayee free and pray:
>
> For his continued walk in repentance and in forgiveness.
>
> That he will successfully break any wrong habits he has formed.
>
> That he will learn to stay free.

Consider praying again for the healing of the person's hurts, wounds, loneliness, confusion, depression or other emotional needs that became apparent during your ministry. Don't hurry this prayer time. Let the Holy Spirit lead you.

Be loving. If there is grief or weeping, comfort the prayee. Put an arm around him if you are a man. Hold her, if you and she are women. Deep healing may still be going on, so don't hurry it. Show love in any appropriate way you can. Don't hesitate to repeat any prayers you made during ministry time as the Holy Spirit leads you. Pray for each of these needs separately, if you have time. Remember that the person is your primary concern and he is probably hurting deeply.

Consider praying for relationships that need healing, such as with a spouse, a parent, a child, an employer. Pray for the Lord to lead him in these relationships, to give him grace, patience, forgiveness, etc.

When praying for the prayee, there is no need for the intercessor or others to avoid touching or talking to the person. He may receive more comfort and healing if more participate in this time of prayer.

Additional spirits may turn up at this stage. For example, the person may dissolve in tears when you start praying healing prayers and by inquiring you find a strong spirit of grief or fear or of something else. These can be dealt with as others were during the ministry time.

CONSIDER KEEPING IN TOUCH WITH THE PERSON YOURSELF TO SEE HOW HE IS DOING AND TO OFFER ENCOURAGEMENT AND PRAYER

The prayee may be deeply touched by your continued caring for him and this alone can be a great encouragement to him.

CONSIDER GIVING THE PRAYEE A SHORT LIST OF WRITTEN SUGGESTIONS ON MAINTAINING HIS FREEDOM

The prayee may be helped if some of your suggestions are set down in written form and given to him to serve as a reminder. You can prepare a written list of the most common suggestions. Things that have been helpful to you personally should be included, and you may want to change the list from time to time as you discover other helpful things that you consider important enough to be included.

A suggested form, called "Maintaining Your Freedom," is set out in **Appendix 3** of this chapter.

Consider whether other things that have surfaced during your ministry should be added to the list for this particular prayee.

NOTES TO THE PERSON MINISTERING

If the prayee is already a mature believer, you may be able to give him quite a lot of help in addition to praying for him. If he is not a mature believer, we must be careful not to overload him with advice and suggestions.

If you have repeated occasions to help people with deliverance, you may want to consider putting down your suggestions for staying free on a page or two of paper that you can give to those you pray for. An example of material you might give the prayee is set out in **Appendix 3** of this chapter. A convenient way to discuss helpful steps with the prayee is to review these pages together with him or her.

Try always to have a fellow pray-er with you. You will benefit from his intercession. He can help listen for the leading of the Holy Spirit. He will be a second person with you in case a serious question arises as to just what happened in the deliverance session.

A prayee may have a friend or relative who brought him to the meeting or he may wish to bring a friend or relative to the private deliverance session. It is often helpful to have such a person present during ministry. Usually the friend or relative is anxious to help the prayee get free and may, if needed, encourage the prayee to cooperate. He or she may also be a key person in helping the prayee stay free after the deliverance. In addition, the friend or relative may be helpful in identifying trouble areas that the prayee has forgotten to mention.

Be a teacher. Help the prayee to see what you are doing – how you locate "open doors", how you close them, how you break the power of any spirit, how you cast it out. Tell the prayee that he can help himself in the future, if need be. (There probably will be a need!) Keep in mind that he may well become a minister himself, in the future, putting into practice what he learns from you.

Remember that you, as a servant of the Lord, having helped someone get free, may come under an attack from Satan. You may encounter sickness, discouragement, difficulty at work or at home, confusion, or tiredness. You can cast away any attacking spirit from yourself. If you can't get the victory on your own, call a friend you trust and ask for prayer.

These feelings can also be intercession, of course. If you are in doubt, ask the Holy Spirit. If they are in fact intercession, use the occasion to pray for the person for whom you believe you are interceding.

Keep your own defenses up:

> Be careful to keep up your normal spiritual activities.
>
> Pray a lot in tongues.
>
> Walk in forgiveness. As a lifestyle!
>
> Walk in repentance. As a lifestyle!
>
> Walk in love, peace and joy!
>
> Keep short accounts with God.
>
> Keep short accounts with your spouse, family, and associates!

Consider every attack of Satan an opportunity to demonstrate the greater power of God! (See James 1:2). Rest in God. Ask Him how to respond to the attack (See James 1:5). Ask Him to defeat Satan for you. He is your strength and deliverer! (See Psalm 18:1, 2, 48)

Keep an eye out for your family!

If Satan cannot get at you, he may try to attack your family.

DELIVERANCE: APPENDIX 1

Some Examples of Areas Where "Doors" May Have Been Opened

RELATIONSHIPS

Father
Mother
Sibling
Spouse
Child
Teacher
Boss, etc.

TRAUMA

Death
Fire
Attack
Divorce
Parent's Divorce, etc.

ADDICTIONS

Drugs
Smoking
Alcohol
Food
Anger
Procrastination
Pornography
Gossip, etc.

SEX OUTSIDE MARRIAGE

Before Marriage
After Marriage
Lust, Fantasy
With same sex
Pornography, Masturbation
Bestiality

CURSES

Intentional
Unintentional
Careless remarks

EMOTIONS, SPIRITS

Resentment, Bitterness
Anger, Hate, Murder
Unforgiveness
Rejection, Loneliness
Despair, Self-pity
Hopelessness
Depression
Fear
Shame, etc.

LONG ILLNESS

SATANIC RITUALS

FREEMASONRY

(Self or in Family)

OCCULT

Fortune Telling
Ouija Board
Horoscopes
Tarot Cards
Palm Reading

HABITUAL SIN

Criticism, Judgement
Pride, Arrogance
Selfishness, Greed
Self-righteousness
Anger, Gossip
Lying, Cheating
Manipulation
Control

OTHERS

Shame, Remorse
Humiliation
Failure, Suicide
Despair, Depression
Hopelessness
Self-Codemnation
Martyrdom, Self-Pity

DELIVERANCE: APPENDIX 2
ANOTHER WAY OF LOOKING AT "AREAS"

An alternative approach to areas is to consider them from the standpoint of body, soul and spirit.

BODY

Sexual sin of any kind

Adultery

Fornication

Pornography, Fantasy, Masurbation

Any homosexual relationship

Bestiality

Uninvited sexual relationship

Incest

Rape

Molestation

Generational Weakness

Addictions

Alcohol

Gluttony

SOUL

Resentment, anger, in all forms

Fear in all forms

Hatred in all forms

Envy in all forms

Unforgiveness, Bitterness

Rejection, Loneliness

Hopelessness, Despair

Pride, Arrogance

Rebellion

Vengeance

Trauma and its effects

Complexes

Fears

Fixations

Greed

Criticism

Gossip

SPIRIT

Any occult experience

Ouija board

Horoscopes

Fortune Telling

Witchcraft

Manipulation

Control

Satanism in any forms

Any pact with Satan

Freemasonry

Freemasonry in family

Curses

Inner Vows

Generational Weakness

NOTE *These lists can be expanded considerably. You may want to make your own additions to them. Make them as useful as you can.*

DELIVERANCE: APPENDIX 3

MAINTAINING YOUR FREEDOM

It is important to understand that remaining free from Satanic bondages is not automatic. It requires vigilance and a sense of purpose on your part. Here are some things you can do to help maintain your freedom.

1. CONSCIOUSLY ALLOW JESUS TO BE LORD (WHOM YOU OBEY!) IN ALL AREAS OF YOUR LIFE

2. MAINTAIN NORMAL PRACTICES FOR A HEALTHY SPIRITUAL LIFE

Keep a daily quiet time.

It is helpful to keep a journal of your thoughts.

Read your Bible daily.

If possible, get into a live Christian fellowship.

Be continually filled with the Holy Spirit. (Ephesians 5:18)

3. TAKE RESPONSIBILITY FOR YOUR THOUGHT LIFE

Don't expect others to fight your battles for you.

Don't be passive.

Don't drift back into old patterns that have caused you trouble before.

4. WALK IN FORGIVENESS AS A LIFESTYLE

Remember, forgiveness is a decision you make not a feeling.

It is important to forgive quickly. No matter how badly you feel hurt.

You may have to forgive someone several times for the same hurt or for different hurts.

5. MAKE RESTITUTION, IF YOU SHOULD

If you cheated someone, repay him.

If you should apologize to someone, do so. (It is best to do this orally.)

If you need to ask forgiveness, ask it!

6. CHANGE YOUR LIFESTYLE, IF YOU SHOULD

If TV is a problem, stop watching it.

If a friend tries to lure you into sin, stop hanging out with him (her).

Consciously address changing bad habits you may have.

Gossip, criticism, over-eating, reading wrong literature, lying... (You can complete your list.)

7. LEARN HOW TO COMBAT TEMPTATION

Sing praise songs, reading Psalms.

Pray vigorously in tongues.

Take authority over harassing spirits and send them away, In the name of Jesus.

When you feel vulnerable, ask others to pray for you.

8. IF YOU FALL, REPENT QUICKLY AND GET THE DOOR CLOSED AGAIN

9. Do "MINI-DELIVERANCES" FOR YOURSELF

If you sense that you are having a problem again or are harassed or tempted, you can give yourself a "mini-deliverance". Look at the door that may have led to your problem. Close it (forgive, repent, ask forgiveness, firmly renounce the action or attitude or spirit involved) and firmly break the power of any spirit involved, in the name of Jesus. Cast out or away any spirit involved in the name of Jesus.

THE FOLLOWING ILLUSTRATION IS TAKEN FROM A NEIL ANDERSON PUBLICATION

One victim of incredible abuse shared this illustration: "It's like being forced to play a game with an ugly stranger in my own home. I kept losing and wanted to quit. But the ugly stranger wouldn't let me. Finally, I called the police (a higher authority) and they came and escorted the stranger out. He knocked on the door trying to regain entry, but this time I recognized his voice and didn't let him in."

DELIVERANCE: APPENDIX 4

QUESTIONNAIRE

Name: _____

Address: _____

Phone: _____

E-mail: _____

Have you been born again?   ☐ Yes ☐ No

If so, briefly describe how and when you became a Christian:

_____

_____

_____

_____

Do you attend church regularly?   ☐ Yes ☐ No

Do you attend a small group?   ☐ Yes ☐ No

Do you have a ministry?   ☐ Yes ☐ No

Do you lead a Bible study?   ☐ Yes ☐ No

Do you teach/preach often?   ☐ Yes ☐ No

Do you pray for the sick?   ☐ Yes ☐ No

Do you sing in a choir?   ☐ Yes ☐ No

Do you serve in church?   ☐ Yes ☐ No

Are you an intercessor?   ☐ Yes ☐ No

Are you a worship leader?   ☐ Yes ☐ No

AREA I. FAMILY RELATIONSHIPS

Please answer the following questions. Where a choice is given, check the correct answer or answers:

YOUR FATHER

Briefly describe your relationship with your father:

_____

_____

Were you friends?   ☐ Yes ☐ No

Was he... (check all that apply)

☐ Warm	☐ Distant	☐ Restrictive	☐ Sickly
☐ Affectionate	☐ Absent a lot	☐ Favor your brothers, sisters	☐ Complaining
☐ Interested in your activities	☐ Aloof		☐ Unduly permissive
☐ Supportive	☐ Punishing	☐ Angry	☐ Honest
☐ Encouraging	☐ Orally abusive	☐ Quarrelsome	☐ Manipulative
☐ Spend time with you	☐ Physically abusive	☐ Fight with your mother	☐ Controlling
	☐ Unfair		

Was he proud of you?   ☐ Yes ☐ No

Explain:

_____

_____

Was he disappointed in you?   ☐ Yes ☐ No

How did he show it?

_____

_____

Was he ashamed of you?   ☐ Yes ☐ No

Explain

_____

_____

Did he discipline you?   ☐ Yes ☐ No

How?

_____

_____

Did he have favorites among the children in your family?   ☐ Yes ☐ No

If so, who were they?

_____

_____

Was he critical of your attitude or ability? ☐ Yes ☐ No

If so, how did he show it?

_____

_____

Did he make any disparaging comments to you about your attitude or ability? ☐ Yes ☐ No

If so, what comments can you remember?

_____

_____

_____

Did he hurt your feelings in any way not discussed above? ☐ Yes ☐ No

Explain

_____

_____

_____

Did your father have habits or qualities you determined you would not have? ☐ Yes ☐ No

If so, explain

_____

_____

_____

_____

_____

Do you have them? ☐ Yes ☐ No

YOUR MOTHER

Briefly describe your relationship with your mother

_____

_____

Were you friends? ☐ Yes ☐ No

Was she... (check all that apply)

☐ Warm	☐ Distant	☐ Unfair	☐ Sickly
☐ Affectionate	☐ Absent a lot	☐ Restrictive	☐ Complaining
☐ Interested in your activities	☐ Aloof	☐ Favor your brothers, sisters	☐ Unduly permissive
☐ Supportive	☐ Punishing	☐ Angry	☐ Honest
☐ Encouraging	☐ Orally abusive	☐ Quarrelsome	☐ Manipulative
☐ Spend time with you	☐ Physically abusive	☐ Fight with your mother	☐ Controlling

Did (do) you feel that she was generally pleased with you?   ☐ Yes ☐ No

How did she show it?

_____

_____

_____

Was she proud of you?   ☐ Yes ☐ No

Explain

_____

_____

_____

Was she disappointed in you?   ☐ Yes ☐ No

How did she show it?

_____

_____

_____

Was she ashamed of you?   ☐ Yes ☐ No

Explain

_____

_____

_____

Did she discipline you?   ☐ Yes ☐ No

How?

_____

_____

_____

Did she have favorites among the children in your family?   ☐ Yes ☐ No

If so, who were they?

_____

_____

_____

Was she critical of your attitude or ability? ☐ Yes ☐ No

If so, how did she show it?

_____

_____

_____

Did she make any disparaging comments to you about your attitude or ability? ☐ Yes ☐ No

If so, what comments can you remember?

_____

_____

_____

Did she hurt your feelings in any way not discussed above? ☐ Yes ☐ No

Explain

_____

_____

_____

Did your mother have habits or qualities you determined you would not have? ☐ Yes ☐ No

If so, explain

_____

_____

_____

Do you have them? ☐ Yes ☐ No

YOUR PARENTS AS A MARRIED COUPLE

How would you describe your parents' relationship with each other?

Were they affectionate with each other? ☐ Yes ☐ No

Were they supportive of each other? ☐ Yes ☐ No

Were they critical of each other? ☐ Yes ☐ No

Did they quarrel or fight in your presence? ☐ Yes ☐ No

Did they divorce? ☐ Yes ☐ No

Did they blame you for their difficulties? ☐ Yes ☐ No

If divorced, have they re-married?

Father ☐ Yes ☐ No

Mother ☐ Yes ☐ No

If so, describe your relationship with your step-parents:

_____

_____

_____

Do you have step-brothers or step-sisters?

If so, describe your relationship with them:

_____

_____

_____

YOUR BROTHERS AND SISTERS

Briefly describe your relationships to your brothers and sisters:

_____

_____

_____

_____

Did you get along well?

If not, describe

_____

_____

_____

Were you proud of them?

Were you ashamed of them?

Were they proud of you?

Were they ashamed of you?

Did they do better than you in some ways?

If so, explain:

_____

_____

Were (are) you jealous of any of them?

If so, why?

_____

_____

Did any of them hurt your feelings in any way not discussed above?

If so, explain.

_____

_____

_____

_____

YOUR FAMILY'S SITUATION

Was your family's income adequate?

Were you ashamed of your family or a family member or of yourself in any way?

Explain.

_____

_____

_____

_____

_____

_____

AREA II. OTHER RELATIONSHIPS

YOUR SCHOOL

Describe your relationship with your schoolmates.

_____

_____

Did (do) you have problems with any of your schoolmates?   ☐ Yes ☐ No

Explain.

_____

_____

Describe your relationship with your teachers.

_____

_____

Did (do) you have problems with any of your teachers?   ☐ Yes ☐ No

Explain.

_____

_____

MILITARY SERVICE

Did (do) your officers treat you fairly?   ☐ Yes ☐ No

If not, explain:

_____

_____

Did (do) your officers hurt your feelings in any way?   ☐ Yes ☐ No

If yes, explain:

_____

_____

Did (do) you get along well with other military people?   ☐ Yes ☐ No

If not, explain:

_____

_____

EMPLOYMENT

Did (do) your employers treat you fairly?   ☐ Yes ☐ No

If not, explain:

_____

_____

Have (do) your employers hurt your feelings in any way? ☐ Yes ☐ No

If so, explain:

_____

_____

Did (do) you get along well with other employees? ☐ Yes ☐ No

If not, explain:

_____

_____

YOUR MARRIAGE [COMPLETE THIS SECTION IF YOU ARE, OR WERE, MARRIED.]

Would you say your spouse is (was)... (Check all that apply)

☐ Warm	☐ Critical	☐ Physically abusive	☐ Manipulative
☐ Affectionate	☐ Uncommunicative	☐ Sickly	☐ Dishonest
☐ Supportive of you	☐ Unfair	☐ Fearful	☐ Controlling
☐ Loving	☐ Quarrelsome	☐ A worrier	
☐ Encouraging	☐ Displeased with you	☐ Lazy	
☐ Loyal	☐ Angry	☐ Alcoholic	
☐ Distant	☐ Orally abusive	☐ Neglectful of duties	

Do (did) you quarrel? ☐ Yes ☐ No

Fight? ☐ Yes ☐ No

Get silent with each other? ☐ Yes ☐ No

Criticize each other? ☐ Yes ☐ No

What are (were) the areas of tension in your relationship?

☐ Money	☐ Raising the kids	☐ Clothes	☐ Your attitude
☐ Chores	☐ Entertaining	☐ Relatives	☐ Your spouse's attitude
☐ Sex	☐ Recreation	☐ Your work	

Do (did) you quarrel or fight in front of the children? ☐ Yes ☐ No

Does (has) your spouse hurt your feelings in things said or done? ☐ Yes ☐ No

If so, explain:

_____

_____

_____

Does (did) your spouse do his/her fair share of household and family duties? ☐ Yes ☐ No

If not, explain:

_____

_____

_____

AREA III. OCCULT INVOLVEMENT

Have you ever tried any of the following activities, seriously or in fun?

☐ Ouija boards   ☐ Fortune Telling   ☐ Horoscopes
☐ Tea leaves   ☐ Tarot Cards   ☐ Palm Reading
☐ Levitation   ☐ Séance   ☐ Other occult things

Have you ever visited or attended:

☐ A Medium   ☐ A Heathen Temple   ☐ Yoga Classes
☐ A Spiritist   ☐ A Fortune Teller   ☐ Martial Arts Training

Have you ever belonged to a secret society?   ☐ Yes ☐ No

If so, which one or ones?_____

Do you now belong?   ☐ Yes ☐ No

To which ones?_____

Have you ever belonged to a satanist cult?   ☐ Yes ☐ No

If so, to which one or ones?_____

Do you now belong?   ☐ Yes ☐ No

To which ones?_____

Have you made any vows to Satan or to a secret society?   ☐ Yes ☐ No

Explain. _____

_____

If so, are you willing to renounce them?   ☐ Yes ☐ No

Have you ever been involved in witchcraft?   ☐ Yes ☐ No

Explain. _____

_____

Has any family member been involved in witchcraft?   ☐ Yes ☐ No

Explain. _____

Have you ever belonged to a Masonic society?   ☐ Yes ☐ No

Have you ever belonged to DeMolay?   ☐ Yes ☐ No

Have you ever belonged to Rainbow girls?   ☐ Yes ☐ No

Have you ever belonged to Eastern Star?   ☐ Yes ☐ No

Do you now belong?   ☐ Yes ☐ No

If so, to which?_____

Do you have any grotesque or hideous Indian, African, or oriental items?   ☐ Yes ☐ No

Have you any object that has been worshipped?   ☐ Yes ☐ No

AREA IV. SEX OUTSIDE OF MARRIAGE

Have you committed fornication (sex before either of you married)? ☐ Yes ☐ No

If yes, a few partners or many?

Was this at your initiative? ☐ Yes ☐ No

Have you committed adultery (you or your partner married)? ☐ Yes ☐ No

If yes, a few partners or many?

Was this at your initiative? ☐ Yes ☐ No

Have you had homosexual relationships? ☐ Yes ☐ No

If yes, a few partners or many?

Was this at your initiative? ☐ Yes ☐ No

Do you now have a fornication, adulterous, or homosexual relationship? ☐ Yes ☐ No

Are you willing to break all such relationships? ☐ Yes ☐ No

Have you been involved with pornography? ☐ Yes ☐ No

Are you now involved with pornography? ☐ Yes ☐ No

How did you get involved?

Are you willing to stop completely? ☐ Yes ☐ No

Do you masturbate frequently? ☐ Yes ☐ No

Have you tried to stop? ☐ Yes ☐ No

Do you consider this a compulsive habit? ☐ Yes ☐ No

Do you have sexual fantasies? ☐ Yes ☐ No

Have you ever molested, raped, or seduced anyone? ☐ Yes ☐ No

Have you ever been molested, raped, or seduced? ☐ Yes ☐ No

Have you ever had sexual contact with an animal? ☐ Yes ☐ No

Is lust a problem for you? ☐ Yes ☐ No

Have you had an abortion? ☐ Yes ☐ No

Have you fathered a child that was aborted? ☐ Yes ☐ No

AREA V. DRUGS

Have you taken illegal drugs? □ Yes □ No

If so, which ones?

_____

_____

_____

_____

Do you take illegal drugs now? □ Yes □ No

If so, which ones?

_____

_____

_____

How did you get started?

_____

_____

_____

_____

_____

_____

_____

_____

_____

_____

_____

Have you sold drugs? □ Yes □ No

AREA VI. TRAUMA

Have you had any traumatic experiences? (Death in family, divorce, dis-charge from work, divorce of parents, auto accident, fire, near-death, rape, death of a child, extreme humiliation, extremely unfair treatment, etc.? ☐ Yes ☐ No

If yes, explain

_____

_____

_____

_____

Do you have nightmares, or hear voices? ☐ Yes ☐ No

If so, when did your nightmares or hearing voices begin?

_____

_____

_____

_____

Do you fear... (Check all that apply)

☐ The dark	☐ Death	☐ Job change
☐ Being alone	☐ Loss of job	☐ Public speaking
☐ Crowds	☐ Flying	☐ Socializing
☐ Small spaces	☐ Loud noise	☐ Failing in your job
☐ Heights	☐ Poverty	☐ Failing in social relationships
☐ Illness	☐ Marriage	☐ Failing in your marriage

When did you begin having these fears?

_____

_____

_____

_____

Do you fear other things? ☐ Yes ☐ No

If yes, explain:

_____

_____

_____

_____

AREA VII. PERSONAL QUALITIES

Are you... (Check all that apply)

☐ A perfectionist	☐ Fearful	☐ Confused	☐ Dishonest
☐ A workaholic	☐ A worrier	☐ Rejected	☐ A glutton
☐ Critical	☐ Nervous	☐ Depressed	☐ Greedy
☐ Reliable	☐ Lazy	☐ Hopeless	☐ Self-righteous
☐ Honest	☐ Careless	☐ Despairing	☐ Shy
☐ Have integrity	☐ Unreliable	☐ Suicidal	☐ Given to self-pity
☐ Proud	☐ A liar	☐ Jealous	☐ Inclined to mention
☐ Manipulative	☐ A cheat	☐ A braggart	unfavorable things
☐ Controlling	☐ A gossip	☐ A complainer	about others

Do you lie? ☐ Yes ☐ No

Tell fibs? ☐ Yes ☐ No

Do you steal? ☐ Yes ☐ No

Keep borrowed items? ☐ Yes ☐ No

Do you have in your possession property that belongs to someone else? ☐ Yes ☐ No

If so, what do you have, and why, and whose is it?

_____

_____

Do you have any habits you consider odd or weird? ☐ Yes ☐ No

If so, explain:

_____

_____

Are you addicted to any habits or substances? (Check all that apply)

Does anyone in your family have addictions? ☐ Yes ☐ No

If so, explain:

_____

_____

Are you sickly? ☐ Yes ☐ No

If so, explain:

_____

_____

AREA VIII. CURSES

Have you engaged in violent quarrels? □ Yes □ No

If so, with whom?

_____

_____

Have you cursed anyone or called anyone names? □ Yes □ No

If so, who and what curses or names?

_____

_____

Has anyone to your knowledge cursed you or called you names? □ Yes □ No

If so, who and what curses or names?

_____

_____

Have you made disparaging remarks about... (Check all that apply)

□ A child of yours	□ Your mother	□ Your pastor	□ Any official
□ Your spouse	□ Other relatives	□ A parishoner	□ Any ethinic group
□ Your siblings	□ An employer	□ A neighbor	□ Others
□ Your father	□ An employee	□ The president	

Have you knowingly placed a hex or curse on anyone, or requested another to do so? □ Yes □ No

If so, explain

_____

_____

Do you sometimes feel that there is a curse on your life? □ Yes □ No

If so, explain:

_____

_____

_____

_____

_____

_____

_____

_____

_____

_____

NOTES

ABOUT
RANDY CLARK

Randy Clark, with a D.Min. from United Theological Seminary, is the founder of Global Awakening, a teaching, healing, and impartation ministry that crosses denominational lines. An in-demand international speaker, he leads the Apostolic Network of Global Awakening and travels extensively for conferences, international missions, leadership training, and humanitarian aid. Randy and his wife, DeAnne, have four grown children who are married with seven grandchildren. They live in Pennsylvania.

THE HEART OF GLOBAL AWAKENING

For all believers everywhere, we present an opportunity to receive power from God. We offer ourselves as evidence that God uses the unqualified when we're willing to take a risk. We strengthen each other through community & theology, and we call out to all those who feel ill-equipped, isolated, and hungry, saying: you belong. To the sick, we offer a community of faith that will believe for your healing. To the skeptic, we offer our stories and our lives as fruit of Jesus' work. Come receive from God what you need, come learn how to take risks in your faith, come join us as we each fulfill God's dream for us. We are a global community of believers empowered to awaken the world.

TO FIND OUT MORE ABOUT GLOBAL AWAKENING VISIT OUR WEBSITE AT:

GLOBALAWAKENING.COM

OTHER BOOKS WRITTEN BY DR. RANDY CLARK

POWER TO HEAL

AUTHORITY TO HEAL

ALMIGHTY IS HIS NAME

THE HEALING BREAKTHROUGH

THERE IS MORE

EYEWITNESS TO MIRACLES

THE SPIRITUAL GIFTS HANDBOOK

BAPTIZED IN THE SPIRIT

THE BIBLICAL GUIDEBOOK TO DELIVERANCE

THE ESSENTIAL GUIDE TO HEALING

FINDING VICTORY WHEN HEALING DOESN'T HAPPEN

THE ESSENTIAL GUIDE TO THE POWER OF THE HOLY SPIRIT

STORIES OF DIVINE HEALING

HEALING ENERGY; WHOSE ENERGY IS IT?

THE HEALING RIVER

SUPERNATURAL MISSIONS

CHANGED IN A MOMENT

ENTERTAINING ANGELS

LIGHTING FIRES

HEALING UNPLUGGED

POWER, HOLINESS, AND EVANGELISM

POWER TO HEAL CURRICULUM

AUTHORITY TO HEAL CURRICULUM

THE ESSENTIAL GUIDE TO HEALING CURRICULUM

globalawakeningstore.com